EXPECT to BELIEVE

**90 Bible Devotionals *to*
Grow Your Faith *for*
the Impossible**

PAUL WILLIAMS

HIGH BRIDGE BOOKS

HOUSTON

Expect to Believe
by Paul Williams

Copyright © 2019 by Life of Faith in Christ Ministries.
All rights reserved.

Printed in the United States of America
ISBN (Paperback): 978-1-940024-81-3
ISBN (eBook): 978-1-940024-82-0

High Bridge Books titles may be purchased in bulk for educational, business, fundraising, or sales promotional use. For information please contact High Bridge Books via www.HighBridgeBooks.com/contact.

Unless specified otherwise, scripture passages taken from the Holy Bible, NEW INTERNATIONAL VERSION®. Copyright © 1973, 1978, 1984 by Biblica, Inc. All rights reserved worldwide. Used by permission. NEW INTERNATIONAL VERSION® and NIV® are registered trademarks of Biblica, Inc.

Published in Houston, Texas by High Bridge Books.

*"And without faith it is **impossible** to please God."*
– Hebrews 11:6, (emphasis added)

Contents

Acknowledgments

I WOULD LIKE TO EXPRESS my appreciation to my loving wife and partner-for-life Michelle for her tireless support and promotion of this book. She is my co-partner in life and ministry in every way.

It is my pleasure to express my appreciation to my friend Kurt Nauck for his editorial work and for his questioning and even for his objections, which contributed to making this book stronger, and to Lucinda Bailey, a dear family friend and a phenomenally talented warrior for Christ on the front lines of the battle for her meticulous and visionary editorial work. This book is substantially better because of their contributions.

Introduction

AT APPROXIMATELY 11:30 A.M. on Tuesday, December 20, 2011 in a hotel room in San Antonio, Texas, God healed me of several significant diseases:

- Sarcoidosis of the lungs—110 nodules in my chest, ranging from 1/8 to 1/4 of an inch in size. Medical prognosis: no treatment and no cure.
- Hemorrhoids
- High cholesterol
- High blood pressure
- Periodic irregular heartbeat

How was I miraculously healed, and what circumstances led up to my healing?

Four months before, my wife Michelle and I enrolled full-time in The Way Bible College.[1] As we studied various subjects—including Biblical Anointing in Christ, Faith 101, Healing 101, Fasting, Worship, and more—my heart burned within me to personally experience a major move of the Holy Spirit in my life.

During a business trip to San Antonio, I returned to my downtown hotel room and began to earnestly study the subject of Biblical healing. Alone in my room, I wrestled with God, attempting to understand why so few miraculous healings occur here in America. In response, the Holy Spirit began pointing me to answers in the Word of God. As I studied and compared scriptures, I began to understand that it is our own ignorance of the Bible, coupled in some cases with our misinterpretation of scripture, which prevent us from understanding our authority in Christ. This blocks us from having the kind of godly faith that moves mountains.

As I saw the scriptures from the Word of God form a chain of letters in my mind not far above my head, I physically reached up with my hands and grabbed the scriptures, exclaiming, "I receive it, Lord!" As I did so, the power of the living God laid me flat on the floor. I was physically helpless for the next four hours as I wept before the Lord and communicated with Him through the Holy Spirit.

When my strength returned, I discovered that so had my health. God had literally rolled back the clock on my physical age by twenty years; I felt and looked like a brand-new man. Later when I visited my doctor of the past seventeen years for a comprehensive physical exam, he could find no trace of my health problems.

More importantly, since then many others have been healed on the spot through the ministry God gave me that day. God wants this for you, Dear Reader, and for all of His believers.

This Bible devotional is a study of the scriptures on Biblical faith and healing from this simple perspective: *What does the Bible say? Don't add anything to it or take anything away.* I pray that, as you read this work, you will discover firsthand—as others have—that, when we act on the Bible in its simplest form for what it says and nothing more, the power of the living God works on our behalf in the form of miraculous, on-the-spot healings, signs, and wonders for the glory of His name.

Finally, to learn what prompted me to produce this devotional book about faith and God's promises, watch the video interview conducted by my covenant partner and wife-for-life, Michelle, on our ministry website at www.LifeOfFaithInChrist.org. We pray you are richly blessed as you read this devotional. Be blessed in the name of Jesus!

---

[1] http://waychurch.org/bible-college/

1

Pursue God Until We Find Him

PURSUING AND MAINTAINING A CLOSE, two-way relationship with God requires a significant level of effort on our part, perhaps more than we may be willing to give at times. Here are several examples from the Bible of just how diligent we must be.

In our first example, notice how an aging Abraham spared no effort to bring what turned out to be three heavenly visitors into his home:

> Abraham looked up and saw three men standing nearby. When he saw them, he hurried from the entrance of his tent to meet them and bowed low to the ground. He said, "If I have found favor in your eyes, my lord, do not pass your servant by." (Gen. 18:2-3)

In our second example, notice what happened when two angels in disguise arrived at the home of Lot in Sodom and Gomorrah:

> "My lords," he said, "please turn aside to your servant's house. You can wash your feet and spend the night and then go on your way early in the morning."

"No," they answered, "we will spend the night in the square."

But he insisted so strongly that they did go with him and entered his house. He prepared a meal for them, baking bread without yeast, and they ate. (Gen. 19:2-3)

In our third example, two of Jesus' disciples strongly pressed Him to stay at their home:

As [two disciples and Jesus] approached the village to which they were going, Jesus continued on as if He was going further. But they urged Him strongly, "Stay with us, for it is nearly evening; the day is almost over." So he went in to stay with them.

When he was at the table with them, he took bread, gave thanks, broke it and began to give it to them. Then their eyes were opened and they recognized him, and he disappeared from their sight. (Luke 24:28-31)

If the disciples had not strongly pressed Jesus to stay with them, they would have missed out on a significant blessing.

In tomorrow's devotional, we will learn about the value of waiting on God to move on our behalf.

2

Waiting on the Lord

SIMPLY PRESSING GOD STRONGLY for His help as we learned yesterday, by itself, may not be enough. To obtain God's help and guidance, we must be also willing to wait for extended lengths of time as may be necessary to receive our answer.

This is vividly illustrated in the book of Jeremiah when the remaining Jews who were not deported to Babylon asked the prophet Jeremiah if they should flee to Egypt for safety to escape vengeance by King Nebuchadnezzar of Babylon. Jeremiah consulted the Lord. Then, he and the people waited ... and waited ... and then waited some more.

Even though the Jews were in a great, big hurry for a decision from God, the days s-l-o-w-l-y passed by with no answer from God. How much time went by? Read for yourself:

> "Pray that the Lord your God will tell us where we should go and what we should do."
>
> "I have heard you," replied Jeremiah the prophet. "I will certainly pray to the Lord your

God as you have requested; I will tell you everything the Lord says and will keep nothing back
from you…"

Ten days later the word of the Lord came to
Jeremiah. (Jer. 42:3-4, 7, emphasis added)

Ten days is a long time when we need an answer from
God quickly. However, it can take even longer than ten days
to hear from God. In this next example, Daniel urgently
sought God by fasting and praying for three weeks before
an angel arrived to interpret a vision God had given to Daniel:

At that time I, Daniel, mourned for three weeks.
I ate no choice food; no meat or wine touched my
lips; and I used no lotions at all until the three
weeks were over …

[Then an angel said to Daniel,] "Do not be
afraid, Daniel. Since the first day that you set
your mind to gain understanding and to humble
yourself before your God, your words were
heard, and I have come in response to them. But
the prince of the Persian kingdom resisted me
twenty-one days. Then Michael, one of the chief
princes, came to help me, because I was detained
there with the king of Persia. Now I have come
to explain to you what will happen to your people in the future, for the vision concerns a time
yet to come." (Dan. 10:2-3, 12-14)

A short recap of my personal testimony from the front
of this devotional is in order. In October 2011, I went on a
strict Daniel Fast for twenty-one days. I gave up television,

prayed constantly, listened to praise and worship music nonstop. I earnestly sought God with every part of my mind, soul, and heart. On the final two days of my twenty-one-day fast, the power of God fell on me in force through visions, signs, miracles, and wonders—all things that had never happened in my life previously. Praise the Lord that I have not been the same since. (That's a good thing!)

God is no respecter of persons. He does not keep the promises in His Word for one person and not another. What God has done for me He will do for you. We know His Word is true and that He does not lie:

> You will seek me and find me when you seek me
> with *all* your heart. (Jer. 29:13, emphasis added)

Let us seek God today with all our heart, soul, and mind. As promised in His Word, we *will* find Him.

Be blessed today in the name of Jesus!

3

Seven Steps to an Intimate Relationship with God

WE OFTEN WISH WE COULD have a closer, more intimate, special relationship with God. However, we seldom do more than wishful thinking to make our desire a reality.

Fortunately, the book of James in the Bible gives us step-by-step directions on how to become intimate with God. Today, we will examine James 4:7-10 sentence-by-sentence, one concept (step) at a time (follow along in your Bibles):

Step 1: "Submit yourselves, then, to God."

Action item: Lord, I want every part of my heart, mind, and soul to be subject to Your will for me. Instruct me, and I commit in advance to do whatever You tell me to do.

Step 2: "Resist the devil, and he will flee from you."

Action item: I take authority over myself, my thoughts, and my actions in the name of Jesus, satan, I rebuke you and the power of your temptations over me in the name of Jesus. You have no power over me.

Step 3: "Come near to God and He will come near to you."

Action item: As told in the Parable of the Prodigal Son, I know that God will run to meet me more than halfway (Luke 15:20). However, the first part of my journey toward God is my decision and my responsibility. I, therefore, commit to pursuing You, God, until I find You (Jer. 29:13).

Step 4: "Wash your hands, you sinners, and purify your hearts, you double-minded."

Action item: I repent of my sins, and I turn away from them. Holy Spirit, examine every part of me and show me where I am wrong and need to change. As You do so, I will change my behavior and not delay or make excuses. I am committed to this process, and I will not slip back from it as I have on other occasions.

Step 5: "Grieve, mourn and wail."

Action item: I mourn for the waste of time I have put myself and You through. I mourn for not being completely serious about my pursuit of You much sooner. I need You more than my daily food, so much so that I have lost much of my interest in food and am fasting to seek Your heart and Your will for me and my life.

Step 6: "Change your laughter to mourning and your joy to gloom."

Action item: I realize the pursuit of You is serious business and requires my full attention. I am fasting to seek Your face. Therefore, I set aside television, sports, games, and any foolishness so that nothing will distract me from what Your Word and Your Spirit are telling me.

Step 7: "Humble yourselves before the Lord, and He will lift you up."

Action item: Everything that I am and everything that I have and will be are yours, O God. I am nothing without You. I pursue You expectantly and hungrily. I claim your promise that those who seek You diligently will find You (Jer. 29:13).

Does this seven-step process spelled out in James 4:7-10 really work? Of course, it does; no surprise there. The Word of God always works when we read it correctly and do our part in faith.

God cannot be pleased without our faith (Heb. 11:6), so we must have faith and expectantly *claim* God's favor and blessing upon us as we earnestly seek Him.

Be blessed today in the name of Jesus!

4

Your Faith Confession Makes Every Difference

IN NUMBERS 14, TEN SPIES defeated themselves through doubt and unbelief. They did not believe God and His promises. Instead, they chose to let the giants and challenges their eyes saw overcome their belief. Notice the Lord's strong reaction to their unbelief:

> The Lord said to Moses, "How long will these people treat me with contempt? How long will they refuse to believe in me, in spite of all the signs I have performed among them? ... So tell them, 'As surely as I live, declares the Lord, I will do to you the very thing I heard you *say*: ... Not one of you will enter the land I swore with uplifted hand to make your home, except Caleb son of Jephunneh and Joshua son of Nun.'"
> (Num. 14:11, 28, 30, emphasis added)

It's interesting to notice that what the spies *spoke* is what they received from God. Ten spies *said* they could not take the land, so they didn't and died in the wilderness. Two spies *said* they could, so they did (Caleb and Joshua).

What does God hear *spoken* in your home and church? Does God hear faith spoken or unbelief? What the majority around you believes is critically important to you because all twelves spies and all of the Israelites suffered for forty years because of the majority's unbelief and lack of faith.

Fellow Believers, I pray God finds faith in your household and congregations.

Be blessed today in Jesus' mighty name.

5

David and Goliath

WHEN DID DAVID WIN HIS VICTORY over Goliath? Was it when David fought the giant or before he even stepped on the battlefield? Let's read God's Word and find out:

> [David to King Saul], "Your servant has killed both the lion and the bear; this uncircumcised Philistine *will be like one of them,* because he has defied the armies of the living God. The Lord who rescued me from the paw of the lion and the paw of the bear *will rescue me* from the hand of this Philistine." (1 Sam. 17:36-37, emphasis added)

My friends, David won his victory before the fight even started by his bold proclamation of *faith* for all to hear.

Notice that David was specific in proclaiming exactly what he expected God to do for him. David publicly proclaimed that God would give him total victory and the death of the giant (v. 36).

Do you pray boldly in faith like this? Do you declare your faith for your family, friends, and all to hear?

If you are accustomed to praying weak, "God-bless-me" type prayers that can mean anything, then begin learning to pray *specifically* and *boldly* and to proclaim your faith aloud with your lips. From one end of the Bible to the other, God's Word is clear that He is pleased by His servants' faith. The bolder our faith is, the bigger His miracles are on our behalf.

Be blessed today in all you do in the name of Jesus!

6

Radical Faith Through What We Say

LET'S GIVE THESE SCRIPTURES CAREFUL CONSIDERATION:

> Joshua said to the Lord *in the presence of Israel*: "Sun, stand still over Gibeon, and you, moon, over the Valley of Aijalon." So the sun ... stopped in the middle of the sky and delayed going down about a full day. There has never been a day like it before or since, a day when *the Lord listened to a human being*. (Josh. 10:12-14, emphasis added)

The last sentence makes it clear that God performed the greatest miracle of all time simply because one of His created human beings had the *bold faith* to publicly ask Him to do so in front of all Israel.

God honors the exercise of our faith! So, how are you praying? Are your prayers specific and bold, or are you praying "safe" prayers that bring little or no results?

I pray your faith will grow radically stronger today in the name of Jesus! Be blessed.

7

Ask, and You Will Receive

WHICH IS EASIER FOR GOD TO DO: to forgive your sins or to physically heal you? For the answer, let us examine two scripture passages:

> Praise the Lord, my soul, and forget not all his
>   benefits—
> who *forgives all your sins* and *heals all your*
>   *diseases*. (Psa. 103:2-3)

> [Jesus said] "Which is easier: to say to this para-
> lyzed man, 'Your sins are forgiven,' or to say,
> 'Get up, take your mat and walk?' But I want you
> to know that the Son of Man has authority on
> earth to forgive sins." So he said to the man, "I
> tell you, get up, take your mat and go home."
> (Mark 2:9)

Both passages imply that God's ability to forgive our sins and His ability to physically heal us involve the same level of effort on His part.

We believe God for our immediate forgiveness of sin when we ask. Likewise, we should also believe God for our immediate physical healing when we ask. God is willing to do either or both, according to what we ask Him in faith.

Be blessed today in Jesus' name!

8

Use the Name of Jesus in Faith

Therefore God exalted him to the highest place and gave him the name that is above every name, that at the name of Jesus every knee should bow, in heaven and on earth and under the earth.

—Philippians 2:9-10

THESE VERSES ARE WORTH MEDITATION. "At the name of Jesus" evil angels, sickness, and disease must surrender. But for this to happen, we believers must speak directly to the problem, using the name of Jesus in faith.

Notice the example of Paul:

> She kept this up for many days. Finally Paul became so annoyed that he turned around and *said to the spirit*, "In the name of Jesus Christ I command you to come out of her!" At that moment the spirit left her. (Acts 16:18, emphasis added)

If we will not boldly use the name of Jesus in *this* manner—that is, speaking directly to the problem in Jesus' name—then we should not be surprised when the power of the living God does not manifest in our lives and circumstances. Use your faith, and do the works Jesus gave you to do in His name! Be blessed today in the name of Jesus.

9

Healing by Faith

*By faith in the name of Jesus, this man whom you see and know was made strong. It is **Jesus' name** and the **faith** that comes through him that has completely healed him, as you can all see.*

—Acts 3:16

IN THIS VERSE, the Apostle Peter lists two reasons why this crippled man was instantly healed: 1) the name of Jesus and 2) the faith that comes through Him. Peter told the crippled man to "rise and walk." Peter then helped the still crippled man up, at which point the man was instantly healed by God (see verse 7).

My friends, Peter boldly put his godly faith *into action* in the full sight of all.

In other words, if we will not ...

1. Ask God for an immediate healing,
2. Proclaim our faith out loud with our lips, and
3. Demonstrate our faith with our bold actions like Peter did.

… then we should not be surprised when God does not perform an immediate, on-the-spot miracle for us. End of story.

Nowhere is the phrase "self-fulfilling prophecy" more applicable than when we exercise our godly, Biblical faith to enable the miraculous on our behalf and for those for whom we pray.

"Such as your faith is, so be it to you." Go and exercise your faith in God's Word today and set a captive of Satan free today in Jesus' mighty name!

Be blessed in the name of Jesus.

10

A Call to Holiness

THE BIBLE MENTIONS *HELL* more than it does *heaven*. Discussions of *sin, wickedness, judgment* and *overcoming* occur repeatedly throughout the New Testament.

Unfortunately, in many Christian churches today, such Biblical topics have gone out of style. Many pastors seldom even *mention*—never mind meaningfully teach on these pervasive Biblical subjects.

The result is a pseudo-love-based doctrine of God's view of our sin. This warped doctrine is taught irrespective of what the inspired Word of God actually says.

But, my friends, the Bible hasn't changed. The Bible still has just as much to say about sin, judgment, overcoming, and holiness as it did when it was written. Here are four scriptures for your careful contemplation today:

> Therefore, since we have these promises, dear friends, let us *purify ourselves* from everything that *contaminates* body and spirit, *perfecting holiness* out of reverence for God. (2 Cor. 7:1, emphasis added)

But just as He who called you is holy, so *be holy in all you do*; for it is written: "Be holy, *because I am holy*." (1 Pet. 1:15-16, emphasis added)

… each person is *tempted* when they are dragged away by their own *evil desire* and *enticed*. Then, after desire has conceived, it gives birth to *sin*; and sin, when it is full-grown, gives birth to *death*. (Jam. 1:14-15, emphasis added)

To those who *by persistence in doing good* seek glory, honor and immortality, he will give eternal life. But for those who are *self-seeking* and who *reject* the truth and follow evil, there will be *wrath* and *anger*. (Rom. 2:7-8, emphasis added)

Join me in praying that the full Word of God will be preached in our congregations and in our communities, not just the parts of the Bible that are popular, "loving," or easy to understand.

Be blessed today in Jesus' name!

11

Overcoming Through Faith

YOU MAY BE ASKING, "Huh? What in the world is 'overcoming through faith'? Is this even possible? Is that biblical?" For the answers, read on. First, notice these three important verses of scripture:

> I have told you these things, so that in me you may have peace. In this world you will have trouble. But take heart! *I have overcome the world.* (John 16:33, emphasis added)

> You, dear children, are from God *and have overcome them*, because the one who is in you is greater than the one who is in the world. (1 John 4:4, emphasis added)

> ... for everyone born of God *overcomes the world.* This is the victory that *has overcome* the world, *even our faith.* (1 John 5:4-5, emphasis added)

Because Jesus has overcome the world, we have overcome the world also. The "catch" or condition, however, is a familiar one: we must first have faith that we already *have* the victory.

If we will not believe that through Christ we *have over-come* the world along with its turmoil and sinful temptations, we will never see full victory in our lives. With this subject as with everything else in the Bible, we must ...

1. Believe the promises in God's Word,
2. Proclaim our belief out loud with our lips,
3. Act on our belief through faith,
4. Repent when we mess up but continue proclaiming victory anyway because scripture says so.

This is a powerful method for overcoming sin and temptation that rapidly yields dramatic results. When done in this manner, you will gain victories over strongholds in your life, victories that you may have been fruitlessly seeking for years until now.

My fellow believers in Christ, in the area of overcoming — as with everything else in the Bible — your faith is powerful and will move the heart of God mightily on your behalf. Don't *try* or *hope* you can overcome. Instead, believe that you *have* overcome and then *speak* God's promises aloud in Jesus' name, and you will overcome as you continue to speak in faith! Your faith spoken aloud for all to hear *precedes* your victory.

Go forth and be victorious today in the mighty name of Jesus!

12

Who We Are in Christ Jesus

*[God] raised Christ from the dead and seated him at his right hand in the heavenly realms, **far above** all rule and authority, power and dominion, and every name that is invoked, not only in the present age but also in the one to come.*

—Ephesians 1:20-21

BECAUSE OF JESUS' SACRIFICE on the cross for us and His resurrection from the dead, God elevated Christ to an all-powerful position at God's right hand, now and for eternity.

Now, are you ready for the incredible part? According to the Bible, where is our standing with our Father God? Notice the astonishing answer in the next chapter:

> And God raised us up with Christ and *seated us with him* in the heavenly realms in Christ Jesus. (Eph. 2:6, emphasis added)

Incredible! We are seated *now* at the right hand of God *with* His Son, Jesus Christ, *far above* all rule and authority, power and dominion, and every name that is named … all through Christ, of course.

If this is true, why then do we Christians so often feel defeated in our daily lives? It's because we have not understood who we are in Christ and what mighty authority we have *now* over evil spirits, sin, wickedness, and every disease. Without this fundamental understanding, we open the door to our own defeat by Satan, sin, and sickness.

I pray today that you will realize and *use* the authority you have in Christ over the names of Temptation, Sin, and Sickness. I pray you are invigorated to new heights in your walk with God.

Set a captive of Satan free today in Jesus' mighty name! You have this authority and responsibility in Christ. Now, *act on your authority* today *through faith* in Jesus' mighty name.

Be blessed in the name of Jesus!

13

Bold Confidence
Through Faith

*For we do not have a high priest who is unable to empathize with our weaknesses, but we have one who has been tempted in every way, just as we are—yet he did not sin. Let us then approach God's throne of grace **with confidence**, so that we may receive mercy and find grace to **help us** in our time of need.*

—Hebrews 4:15-16

NOTICE THAT OUR FATHER GOD isn't merely *letting* us come before Him with our requests, but rather that He actually *expects* us to seek His help. Not only that, He wants us to ask with *confidence*. Pretty amazing concept... isn't it?

So, how then is your faith? Could it be that you see yourself as having such a low-standing before God that daring to ask Him to heal yourself or others has become a great big request in your eyes?

If so, is it any wonder then that you are defeated before you even ask?

The Bible is clear that we, as believers, are seated *with Christ* at the right hand of the Father *far above* evil spirits, sin, and sickness. As such, God *wants* us—no, He *expects* us—to come before Him in *confidence*.

Go and exercise your *bold faith* today in the name of Jesus!

14

How to Increase Your Faith

EACH EXERCISE OF OUR FAITH leads us to a greater challenge. God will steadily grow our faith provided we let Him and follow His lead in our lives.

Here is an example from scripture:

> Then the Lord said to [Moses], "What is that in your hand?"
>
> "A staff," he replied.
>
> The Lord said, "Throw it on the ground."
>
> Moses threw it on the ground and it became a snake, and he ran from it. Then the Lord said to him, "Reach out your hand and take it by the tail." So Moses reached out and took hold of the snake and it turned back into a staff in his hand. (Exod. 4:2-4)

To throw the staff down because God said so took only a little faith. However, to pick the staff back up because God said so took a lot more faith because the staff was a snake at that moment. Nevertheless, Moses was able to do so because the first small exercise of his faith prepared him for the next, larger exercise of his faith.

God will do the same for us in our lives if we will let Him. At every step, especially the first step, we have a choice to make. We must exercise the little faith we have in order to receive more faith. If you won't or don't exercise the small amount of faith you already have, you risk losing even that.

This godly principle of "use it or lose it" is illustrated in Jesus' Parable of the Talents. The servant equipped with only one talent had it taken away from him because he failed to use it wisely:

> For whoever has will be given more, and they will have abundance. Whoever does not have, *even what they have will be taken from them.*
> (Matt. 25:29)

I agree that this may seem harsh. Nevertheless, this is a divine principle for our own good that none of us can alter or escape.

As the saying goes, "use it or lose it." Allow God to grow your faith today by using it in Jesus' name!

15

God Responds to Our Faith

FOR THOSE OF YOU STILL WAITING for more "proof" that our prayers can and do indeed move the heart of God into action on our behalf simply because we ask in faith, this scripture is for you:

> This is what the Lord says — your Redeemer, who
>   formed you in the womb:
> I am the Lord, the Maker of all things, who
>   stretches out the heavens, who spreads out the
>   earth by myself ...
> who *carries out* the words of his servants and *ful-*
>   *fills* the predictions of his messengers ...
>   (Isa. 44:24-26, emphasis added)

There it is. Wait no longer.

However, for those who are determined not to believe that it is our faith that moves God into action on our behalf, no scripture in the Bible will ever be enough to change their minds, including the passage above. Why is this?

As we learned in yesterday's message, we inevitably *lose* our faith unless we *use* it. Sadly, once our faith is completely gone, our ability to believe God for anything, including for faith, is blocked by the sin of unbelief. We find ourselves crippled in our lives and ministries because of this serious sin due to the difficulty of recognizing and overcoming this condition once we are trapped in it.

Of course, most certainly God will restore anyone who repents, confesses, and turns away from sin. Short of this, however, there is no way back for those trapped by this sin.

As you go about your daily life today, I encourage you to thank God that your heart is still open to His Word, the Bible. Then, go further and ask God to help you to *use* your faith today so it can grow, rather than allowing it to stagnate and shrink from continued lack of use.

My friends, all around us are the lost, sick, weary, and dying. I pray that the compassion and love of our Father God will settle upon your heart and open your eyes wide to the ripe mission field all around us.

It's time to act. Use your faith today and set a captive of Satan free in the mighty name of Jesus!

16

God's Plan for Us

LIFE UNDER THE OLD TESTAMENT Mosaic Law of the Bible was based on obedience. In contrast, life under the New Testament is founded on grace, love, and faith.

> Clearly no one who relies on the law is justified before God, because "the righteous will live by faith." The law is not based on faith; on the contrary, it says, "The person who does these things will live by them." (Gal. 3:11-12)

This next scripture passage nicely contrasts the differences between life under the Old and New Testaments:

> Before the coming of this *faith*, we were held in *custody* under the law, locked up until the *faith* that was to come would be revealed. So the law was our *guardian* until Christ came that we might be *justified by faith*. Now that this *faith* has come, we are no longer under a guardian.
>   So in Christ Jesus you are all children of God *through faith*. (Gal. 3:23-26, emphasis added)

Here's a nice way of summing up God's plan for us because of the victory won by Jesus. We are justified by *faith* through *grace* to walk in *love*.

If we neglect or minimize any one of these three vital principles, we may as well return to life under the Old Testament Law.

Today, we most frequently struggle with *love* and *faith*. Let's ask God today for His strength to apply all three so that we can become the obedient Christ-followers He desires.

Live a life of victory today in Jesus' name!

17

Perseverance Through Trials

Dear friends, do not be surprised at the fiery ordeal
that has come on you to test you, as though
something strange were happening to you. But
rejoice in as much as you participate in the sufferings
of Christ, so that you may be overjoyed when his
glory is revealed.

—1 Peter 4:12-13

IN THIS SCRIPTURE PASSAGE, we see yet another aspect of living our lives by faith. In the midst of our trials, we must have faith that God sees our struggles and pain and will lead us through to the other side. Not only this, we must also believe that God will use our every situation for our good. Let's take a look.

> And we know that *in all things* God works for the good of those who love him, who have been called according to his purpose. (Rom. 8:28)

We must claim by faith God's promise that He will turn our negative experiences into something good for us in His own good way, will, and time. If we don't believe God will do this for us, then we tie His hands through our fear and lack of trust.

May our loving Father God richly bless you today in the name of our Lord and Savior Jesus!

18

How to Help Others with the Faith for Their Miracle (and Boost Your Own Faith)

NOTICE HOW JESUS WORKED to grow the faith of a father who needed a miracle for his demon-possessed son before Jesus performed the needed miracle:

> " [The demon] has often thrown [my son] into fire or water to kill him. *But if you can do anything,* take pity on us and help us."
>
> "*If you can?*" said Jesus. "Everything is possible for one who believes."
>
> Immediately the boy's father exclaimed, "*I do believe*; help me overcome my unbelief!"
> (Mark 9:22-24, emphasis added)

Likewise, before you pray for healing of others, pay close attention to the words they use when they request your intercession. When we pray for those who speak unbelief, even innocently, God cannot move on their behalf, and no miracle will occur. Then, their faith drops further, making it even more difficult to intercede for them the next time around. Not good.

Instead, much like Jesus did, first work to raise their faith as necessary. I do this by quoting scriptures from the Bible and by sharing how God healed me. After all, we know that "faith cometh by hearing, and hearing by the word of God" (Rom. 10:17, KJV).

Once their faith confession is right, I agree with their request in the name of Jesus. God keeps His Word, so it is no wonder then that God performs their miracle according to the faith that they have expressed.

Of course, first be sure to start with yourself. Our words reflect the confession of our hearts. Is your faith confession right? If not, make sure your own faith in the Word of God is there and that your own confession is right before you work to grow someone else's faith.

Go set a captive of Satan free today in the mighty name of Jesus! Don't keep "thinking about it." It's time to do it.

Be blessed today in the name of Jesus!

19

Edifying Others
Through What We Say

*Do not let any unwholesome talk come out of your mouths, but only what is **helpful for building others up** according to their needs, that it may **benefit** those who listen.*

—Ephesians 4:29

HOW OFTEN DO YOU follow this scripture? How do you reply when fellow believers come to you who need God's intervention in their lives in some way or physical healing in their bodies? Do you respond with a generic, safe reply such as, "Brother or Sister, I will pray for you"?

Or, do you use your faith and reply, "My God will meet all your needs according to the riches of his glory in Christ Jesus"? (Phil. 4:19)

What we say out loud with our lips makes all the difference to God. Re-read Ephesians 4:29 above. Which response *builds up* and *benefits* your fellow believer in need? A safe response? Or, praying God's Word over the situation to edify the person in need and to edify yourself as well in the process?

People are in need are all around us. Pray for God to open your eyes to someone you can encourage, bless, and edify today in Jesus' name!

20

God's Ten Conditions for His Miraculous Response to Our Prayers

HERE IS A LIST OF GOD'S ten conditions that enable Him to act miraculously on our behalf in response to our requests. We must ask God ...

- With right motives in our hearts (Jam. 4:2b-3)
- According to God's will (1 John 5:14—see the final lesson of this book for complete information.
- In faith derived from hearing the Word of God (Rom. 10:17)
- If we remain in Jesus and Jesus' words remain in us (John 15:7)
- Without harboring known sin in our hearts (1 John 3:22; Matt. 15:7)
- If a man, being considerate and respecting our wives "so that nothing will hinder [our] prayers" (1 Pet. 3:7)
- While bearing fruit in God's Kingdom (John 15:16)

- In agreement with another believer, which in practical reality is often the person you are praying for (Matt. 18:19)
- Proclaiming our bold faith out loud with our lips (2 Cor. 4:13)
- Believing *we have* received our miracle *before* we receive it (Mark 11:24; 2 Cor. 5:7; and Acts 3:6-7)

Does this seem like a lot of conditions to you? If so, think again. Recall the pages of "fine print" terms you must sign in order to purchase the car you drive or the home you live in. It's interesting that, for these earthly treasures, we are willing do whatever is necessary to get what we need.

Likewise, we must be willing do whatever is necessary to gain heavenly treasure as well.

In fact, let's go even further. Learn to think of God's ten conditions as merely being the submitted life under God and His Holy Spirit that we, as Christian believers, should have been living all along. With this viewpoint, God's terms will not seem like burdensome conditions at all, but rather as a description of the normal Christian life we have been living all along.

For some of us, this may be a whole new way of looking at this. Meditate and pray about this as you continue to study God's Word. I pray you will decide to take your walk with God to new heights. All things are possible for those who earnestly seek God with all their heart, mind, and soul!

Be blessed in Jesus' mighty name!

21

Zeal for God

HERE ARE SEVERAL SCRIPTURES for your contemplation today:

My soul yearns, even faints, for the courts of the
  Lord;
my heart and my flesh cry out for the living
  God. (Psa. 84:2)

… zeal for your house consumes me, and the insults of those who insult you fall on me.
(Psa. 69:9)

[As Jesus cleanses the temple] His disciples re-
membered that it is written: "Zeal for your house
will consume me." (John 2:17)

All of us know how excited we can become about a
sports game, a pay raise or promotion at work, a new car, or
a new home. Our celebration can be enthusiastic, and we
will call, text, email, or Facebook our friends far and wide to
let them know about our earthly good news.

Yet, when it comes to the ultimate Good News of the
universe—the news of our salvation and the coming return
of Jesus to this earth—oddly we are far more subdued. The

average Christian can go weeks, months, or longer without saying anything meaningful about their faith to a fellow believer, never mind sharing Christ with the lost, sick, and dying all around us.

Why is this? Could it be that our priorities are misplaced? Or, could it be that Jesus and His heavenly reward for us are not as real to us as they should be? Or, have we forgotten—or, perhaps no longer care—that the unsaved all around us will go to hell if we do not reach them?

I believe the answer is a combination of all three. Whatever the reason may be, my prayer for all of us today is that we will repent of our misplaced zeal and reprioritize what is most important to us.

Pray today that you are consumed by the fire of the Holy Ghost, zeal for the Lord's house, and His love for the lost in Jesus' mighty name! What we earnestly seek from God in faith is what we will receive! Ask, and you *will* receive.

Blessings in Christ!

22

Conquering Unnatural Fear That Can Hinder Your Faith

LET'S EXAMINE THIS SUBJECT by studying the way Job prayed for his household:

> ... [Job] would sacrifice a burnt offering for each of [his children], thinking, "Perhaps my children have sinned and cursed God in their hearts." This was Job's *regular custom*. (Job 1:5, emphasis added)

At first glance, Job's prayer for his kids appears to be a wonderful, proactive example for us to follow. But later on in the book of Job, we learn Job's reaction to the disasters God allowed satan to inflict on him and his children:

> [Job said], "What I feared has come upon me;
> what I dreaded has happened to me."
> (Job 3:25)

Now, we can see that Job had acted out of unnatural fear for his children rather than out of trust in God.

How do you pray for your children and loved ones? Contrast these two very different prayer approaches:

Prayer 1: "Lord, save my children from hell, poverty, and sickness. I am so afraid they are on the wrong track. Don't let the devil get them!"

Prayer 2: "Father God, based on your Word (quote scriptures here), I claim salvation, prosperity, and health for my children in the name of your Son, Jesus. Your Word says it, and I believe it!" Then speaking out loud directly to Satan, declare, "I rebuke your influence over my children in the mighty name of Jesus!"

The first prayer is the unwitting result of unnatural fear and lack of faith in God's promises in His Word. This type of prayer can actually open the door for an attack by the demonic and the entrance of the very things we fear most.

The second prayer expresses faith and trust in God's Word. This type of prayer of faith and follow up action opens the door for God's miraculous blessing and provision and takes Biblical authority over the power of the demonic.

Here are two scriptures on the subject of fear we should meditate on and know well:

I will not fear though tens of thousands assail
   me on every side. (Psa. 3:6)

Even though I walk through the darkest valley,
I will fear no evil, for you are with me;
your rod and your staff, they comfort me.
(Psa. 23:4)

Beginning today, let's make a habit of exercising faith in all we do, say, and pray. God is pleased by and responds to our faith!

Be blessed in Jesus' name.

23

Conquering Obstacles in Our Path

THE CHRISTIAN WALK WITH GOD isn't all triumphs and good times. It also includes trials, sacrifices, suffering, and overcoming. Notice …

> For it has been granted to you on behalf of Christ not only to believe in him, but *also to suffer for him.* (Phil. 1:29, emphasis added)

> [Jesus said,] *"In this world you will have trouble. But take heart! I have overcome the world.* (John 16:33, emphasis added)

From time to time in life, each of us will face our own "Red Sea" obstacle, our own Goliath the Giant challenge, or our own Jordan River flood-stage crossing. However, it is what we say and do in reaction to our obstacles that will either allow God to miraculously intervene on our behalf or leave us struggling on our own.

So, how *should* we react to challenges?

First, notice how the two faithful spies, Caleb and Joshua, publicly proclaimed victory in advance in reaction to the discovery of giants in the land of Canaan:

... do not be afraid of the [giants] of the land, because we will devour them. Their protection is gone, but the Lord is with us. *Do not be afraid of them*. (Num. 14:9, emphasis added)

Next, notice how Jesus tells us to take action by directly rebuking our problems:

[Jesus said,] "If you have faith as small as a mustard seed, *you can say to this mountain*, 'Move from here to there,' and it will move. *Nothing* will be impossible for you." (Matt. 17:20, emphasis added)

Last, here's Jesus' description of what our *daily* faith walk should look like:

[Jesus said,] "Therefore *do not worry about tomorrow*, for tomorrow will worry about itself. Each day has enough trouble of its own." (Matt. 6:34, emphasis added)

So, here we have it:

- In faith, proclaim victory in advance with your lips.
- Speak directly to and rebuke your problems in the name of Jesus.
- Do not worry about tomorrow (a major act of faith). Instead, wait patiently on the Lord.

God gives signal victories to us over our obstacles both large and small when we operate in bold faith in this manner. Tomorrow, we will look at some examples of God's miraculous power in a variety of everyday circumstances.

God loves you with a passion and an intensity that can be difficult to even conceive, never mind fully understand.

Be blessed, My Fellow Believers, in the name of Jesus!

24

God Will Perform Miracles for You If You Will Ask

*[Jesus speaking] I chose you and appointed you so that you might go and bear fruit—fruit that will last—and so that **whatever** you ask in my name the Father will give you.*

—John 15:16

BASED ON THE PROMISE in this scripture, you may ask just what can we pray for besides healing? Answer: *anything* at all that you need according to the Spirit of God. As examples, I *immediately received* these miracles by quietly to myself asking God to ...

1. Quiet a bothersome cell phone so I could witness without distraction to a business owner. Although he tried several times, he was unable to get his phone to work—the screen appeared dark and the phone seemed dead. However, immediately after I finished witnessing to him, his phone lit up and began

ringing and working normally without being touched.

2. Have everyone leave a noisy room at an individual's workplace so I could witness to a certain person in peace. Right after I prayed, everyone left the room and stayed gone until I finished witnessing in about twenty minutes, after which they all returned without being called.

3. Have an individual at work I did not know leave a group of others for an isolated area so I could witness to that person in peace.

4. Prevent anyone from getting on a bus until I had finished witnessing to its driver. While she parked and waited at a series of busy bus pickup stops full of people, she became puzzled that no one was boarding. I remained the sole passenger for about thirty minutes while God used me to mightily awaken her faith. She rededicated herself to the study of His Word and was praising God as I departed her bus!

How exactly do I pray in such situations? As an example, while ministering to someone whom God leads me to, I typically put my hand over my mouth as I very quietly pray, "Father God, send this person's doubting co-worker, etc. away, and do not allow him to return until I have finished witnessing and praying with this man about your only Son,

Jesus Christ." That's it. The co-worker will immediately get up, leave and stay gone until I am done.

Why? Because God is pleased with our bold faith and because He has promised in His Word to do *whatever* we ask Him to do in His Son Jesus' name. That's why. A lot of faith isn't required. All we have to do is simply believe God's Word is true and then *act* on it. That's it.

My Fellow Believers, this leaves us with no excuse for not witnessing to those we meet. Go set a captive of Satan free today in the mighty name of Jesus!

25

Blessed Are Those Who Believe Without Seeing

DESPITE EVERYTHING JESUS had taught His disciples foretelling his death and resurrection in three days, and the eye-witness testimony of other disciples who testified that Jesus was alive, notice this intense expression of unbelief from Jesus' disciple, Thomas:

> [Thomas said] "Unless I see the nail marks in his hands and put my finger where the nails were, and put my hand into his side, *I will not believe.*"
>
> Then [Jesus appeared to His disciples] and said to Thomas, "Put your finger here; see my hands. Reach out your hand and put it into my side. *Stop doubting and believe.*"
>
> Thomas said to him, "My Lord and my God!"
>
> Then Jesus told him, "Because you have seen me, you have believed; blessed are those who have not seen and yet have believed."
> (John 20:25, 27-29, emphasis added)

Ouch! My friends, it would be easy to believe if God Himself were to appear to us in person and answer all of our questions about faith, healing, miracles, and whatever else we want answered before asking us to believe. But Jesus has already told us what He is going do in response to our need for "proof":

> [Jesus] sighed deeply and said, "Why does this generation ask for a sign? Truly I tell you, *no sign will be given to it.*" Then he left them, got back into the boat and crossed to the other side. (Mark 8:12-13, emphasis added)

Ouch again. I pray we do not cause Jesus to sigh heavily over our unbelief as He did over the Jews 2,000 years ago. Instead, let's learn from their failures. In the words of Jesus in John 20:27, "*Stop doubting and believe.*" Have faith in God, His Word, and His promises and *believe!*

Once you truly and deeply *believe*, it becomes easy to *act* on your belief and see God respond miraculously on your behalf.

Blessings in Christ!

26

Faith in the Earth

AT THE END OF JESUS' PARABLE about the unjust judge, Jesus appears to ask a rhetorical question:

> ... when the Son of Man comes, *will he find faith on the earth*? (Luke 18:8b, emphasis added)

Digging deeper into this subject, we see that men of strong faith existed throughout the Old Testament:

> [Faith] is what the *ancients* were commended for. (Heb. 11:2, emphasis added)

The ancients listed in Hebrews 11 died without ever seeing the hoped-for, promised Messiah, Jesus Christ, whom we are richly blessed with:

> [The ancients] were all *commended for their faith*, yet none of them received what had been promised since God had planned *something better for us*. (Heb. 11:39-40a, emphasis added)

Faith should be even easier for us! We New Testament believers clearly have the far better end of God's power and promises, as indicated in this scripture:

Whereby are given *unto us* exceeding great and precious *promises*: that *by these* ye might be *partakers of the divine nature,* having escaped the corruption that is in the world through lust.
(2 Pet. 1:4, KJV, emphasis added)

But we must understand that God's "exceeding great and precious promises" are only valid if they are believed through faith. Our faith is vitally important because we are told,

Without faith it is *impossible* to please God.
(Heb. 11:6, emphasis added)

Fellow believers, it should be easier for us to believe God's promises than it was prior to Christ's first coming! However, Jesus' question in Luke 18 appears to indicate that there will be a pervasive lack of faith in these end times we are living in today. This seems increasingly apparent in today's society.

But not in our households! May each of us earnestly pray that, when Jesus returns to Earth, He will find abundant faith operating in our lives, families and churches.

Be blessed today!

27

Asking God Versus Rebuking Satan

TODAY, LET'S CLEAR UP what may at first seem to be a contradiction in the scriptures over how to obtain effective results from God. First, notice the seemingly very different approaches to problem resolution in the following two passages:

> [Jesus said,] "Very truly I tell you, my Father will give you whatever you *ask in my name*."
> (John 16:23, emphasis added)

> [Jesus said] "... if you have faith as small as a mustard seed, you can *say to this mountain*, 'Move from here to there,' and it will move. Nothing will be impossible for you." (Matt. 17:20, emphasis added)

So, which is it? Should we pray asking God for His help, or should we take charge over the situation ourselves?

The answer can be either or sometimes both, depending on the circumstances involved. Specifically, we must always ask God for His help, but at the same time, we must always take authority ourselves through Jesus' name to rebuke Satan and all of his manifestations and afflictions.

Say what, you ask? Here are some clarifying examples:

1. Though we should always ask God to bless us, it is our job to rebuke Satan in the name of Jesus. God didn't instruct us to ask Him to resist the devil for us. Rather, God instructed *us* to "resist the devil, and he will flee from you" (Jam. 4:7). *We* must do the resisting ourselves, always and only in the name of Jesus.

2. Though we are to ask God for health, it is our job to rebuke disease and sickness ourselves using, again in the mighty name of Jesus.

3. Though we are to ask God for prosperity, it is our job to rebuke poverty, lack, and the destroyer. Though God has not promised us a life of ease, He has promised to meet our needs.

4. Though we are to ask God for direction, it is our job to rebuke confusion, division, acrimony, etc.

Again, the right course of action to take in any given situation can be either or both, depending on the situation. We can rely upon the Holy Spirit to guide us with perception and wisdom as our walk with God progresses and as we learn to hear and obey His voice.

Be blessed today in the mighty name of Jesus!

28

Overcoming Doubt That Can Hinder Your Faith

IF YOU SUDDENLY REALIZE just how terribly sick someone really is while praying for their healing, don't let the devil tell you that you are "doubting" and therefore trick you into thinking you lack enough faith for that person's healing. You aren't doubting; you are just recognizing reality in the natural.

Recognizing "reality" in the natural is different than doubting the promises of God in His Word. Let's see how Abraham handled reality checks.

> Without weakening in his faith, [Abraham] *faced the fact* that his body was as good as dead—since he was about a hundred years old—and that Sarah's womb was also dead. Yet he *did not waver through unbelief* regarding the promise of God, but was *strengthened* in his faith and gave glory to God, being *fully persuaded* that God had power to do what he had promised. This is why "it was credited to him as righteousness." (Rom. 4:18-24, emphasis added)

In verse 19, we see that we must not let circumstances dictate our faith. Rather, we must believe God's promises all the more (verse 20).

When it looks impossible from a human perspective, the stage is now set for God and God alone to act. This should encourage us all the more to lean on God's promises and expect the miracle we need from God.

> But when you ask, you must believe and not doubt. (Jam. 1:6-8)

Go set a captive of Satan free today in the name of Jesus!

29

Don't Let Pride
Interfere with Your Faith

GOD WILL NOT WORK miracles through us if we are prideful. Being proud of ourselves or our accomplishments means that we do not recognize God alone as being the sole Author of all that is good that we accomplish. For this reason, our pride interferes with our reliance on God and even with our rationale for the exercise of our faith. This prevents God from granting our requests.

So, how can we prevent ungodly pride? Pride is something I have frequently struggled with in my life and am still regularly tempted with its snare. Today, I would like to share with you how the Lord is leading me to overcome in this area.

First, recognize that God hates pride with a passion:

> The Lord detests all the proud of heart.
> Be sure of this: They will not go unpunished.
> (Prov. 16:5)

Next, be aware that we can do *nothing at all*—however small it may be—without God first enabling us to do it:

... no one can say, "Jesus is Lord," except by the Holy Spirit. (1 Cor. 12:3b)

I read this verse a lot. It is always a very humbling thought for me.

Here is another one:

... for it is *God who works in you* to will and to act in order *to fulfill his good purpose.* (Phil. 2:13, emphasis added)

This verse makes me realize that nothing good I do is my idea or my doing but is rather orchestrated by God through me for His glory. I am just the vessel He uses to accomplish His will.

Last, recognize anew the role of godly humility in our daily walk with the Lord through these two scriptures:

For all those who exalt themselves will be humbled, and those who humble themselves will be exalted. (Luke 14:11)

Humility is the fear of the Lord;
its wages are riches and honor and life.
(Prov. 22:4)

My prayer today is that we let nothing interfere with our reliance on God alone and the exercise of our faith, "for without faith it is impossible to please God" (Heb. 11:6). Now, join me in putting into practice what we have learned.

Be blessed today in Jesus' name!

30

Worthiness Before God to Ask for Your Miracle

AT TIMES, IT CAN BE difficult for me to feel worthy enough before God to have the kind of bold faith God requires so He can perform miracles on our behalf. When such times occur, I find it helpful to remember God's unconditional love for me (make these scriptures personal to yourself):

> But because of his *great love* for us [me], God, who is rich in mercy, made us [me] alive with Christ *even when we were [I was] dead in transgressions*—it is by *grace* you [I] have been saved. (Eph. 2:4-5, emphasis added)

> But now [God] has reconciled you [me] by Christ's physical body through death to present you [me] *holy* in his sight, *without blemish* and *free from accusation*. (Col. 1:22, emphasis added)

What amazing love and divine favor ... isn't it? But the next verse contains an important condition we must abide by (personalize the following passages on your own):

If you continue in your *faith,* established and firm, and do not move from the hope held out in the gospel. (Col. 1:23, emphasis added)

How can we continue in *faith*? By fixing our eyes on Jesus. Jesus lived as a man here on this earth, but fully overcame fear and doubt (Heb. 4:15). So much so, in fact, that it is written that Jesus actually *authored* faith:

... fixing our eyes on Jesus, the *pioneer and perfecter of faith.* (Heb. 12:2a, emphasis added)

Add up all these great and precious promises, and now we should *expect* help from our loving Daddy, Father God:

The Spirit you received does not make you slaves, so that you live in fear again; rather, the Spirit you received brought about your adoption to *sonship.* And by him we cry, "Abba, Father." (Rom. 8:15, emphasis added)

When we move beyond *hoping* for God's help to *expecting* God's help simply because we asked in faith in the name of Jesus, we release God to do dramatic signs, wonders and miracles on the spot through us.

From one end of the Bible to the other, we see that God responds to our faith. As in the life of Joshua, the bolder our faith, the more dramatically God can move on our behalf.

Go set a captive of Satan free today in the name of Jesus!

31

What We Say Will Make or Break Us

READ THIS CAREFULLY:

> If you *say*, "The Lord is my refuge," and you
>   make the Most High your dwelling,
> no harm will overtake you, no disaster will
>   come near your tent …
> "Because he loves me," says the Lord, "I will
>   rescue him; I will protect him, for he
>   acknowledges my name.
> He will call on me, and I will answer him; I will
>   be with him in trouble, I will deliver him and
>   honor him.
> With long life I will satisfy him and show him
>   my salvation." (Psa. 91:9-10, 14-16, emphasis
>   added)

The word *say* in verse 9 means more than simply praying for the Lord's protection periodically and then thinking we're good to go when disaster or crisis arises. Rather, verse 9 means exactly what it says: *speak aloud* our trust and faith in God's supernatural, protective power every time trouble arises … which it will.

It's easy enough to have faith in God's promises before trouble threatens, but what happens when we are unexpectedly confronted with a crisis? That's when proclaiming our bold faith aloud counts the most. But sadly, that's also when we are instead most likely to speak words of doubt, fear, confusion, hurt, and unbelief. When a crisis strikes, our tendency is to work hard to first understand all of the details and even halfway control the situation before we then begin to have "faith" that God will intervene on our behalf. But is that really faith?

Godly faith boldly proclaims aloud our complete trust in God's deliverance and providence at the first sign of trouble before we know all of the gory details or halfway figure out what to do.

Godly faith proclaims from the start, "The Lord is my refuge and strength! I claim God's promise in Psalm 91 that this disease [substitute your crisis here] will not touch my family in the name of Jesus!"

From personal experience, I can share with you that God works dramatic miracles and moves mountains on our behalf when we speak aloud our bold faith for all to hear. Go and tell your unbelieving friends what Jesus will do for you before He does it. The impact of your witness to them after that will be immensely more effective.

Be blessed today in the name of Jesus!

32

Instant Miracle:
A Healing Testimony

GOD IS ABLE AND WILLING to do for you what he did for me. This is a testimony of how God miraculously healed me of a skin infection on both of my legs. Here's how it happened.

First, as the pain steadily grew, I knew that my words were powerful. I knew that I could either speak my faith into the situation, or by my silence or complaining, I could unwittingly confirm the power of the disease over me. Read carefully:

> It is written: "I *believed*; therefore I have *spoken*." Since we have that same spirit of faith, we also *believe* and therefore *speak*. (2 Cor. 4:13, emphasis added)

So I applied these verses to my situation by *first* speaking aloud my faith with my lips that God would heal me on the spot. I proclaimed my faith that I would be healed *before* I said a word to anyone else. Normally, I would have run to my wife to complain to her first for 10 minutes before finally getting around to praying about it. Sound familiar?

Next, I simply prayed, "Father, God, I receive your Son's finished work on the cross of healing for my legs. It is done in the name of Jesus. Thank you, Father, for healing me!"

I knew that I was healed because of these scriptures:

[Jesus said,] "Therefore I tell you, whatever you ask for in prayer, believe that you *have received it*, and it will be yours." (Mark 11:24, emphasis added)

For we live by faith, not by sight [or by feeling]. (2 Cor. 5:7, my words added)

So, I continued praising God and kept going without seeking any treatment for my legs despite the pain because I *knew* I was healed by faith.

But within thirty minutes, I realized that my legs were not healed. In fact, the pain had actually increased. So, in meditation with God through the Holy Spirit, I soon realized the reason why God had not heard my prayer. My prayer for healing had been robotic—an empty formula, so to speak. It had consisted of mere words spoken *at* God rather than *to* God—or, far more powerfully yet, *with* God as part of precious, two-way communication with Him through the Holy Spirit.

So, I immediately began communing in the sweet Holy Spirit with our Father God (those who have the Gift of the Holy Spirit will understand). This time, I *saw* in the Spirit, by faith, Him who sits on the throne forever and ever, the mighty, living, and eternal God who fills all heaven and earth with His glory, majesty, and power.

Physically overwhelmed and filled to the overflowing with unspeakable awe and wonder, I cried out, "Forgive me, Father, for my earlier casual prayer. I receive the healing You have for me in the mighty name of Your only Son, Jesus Christ!"

Instantly, I was healed. All I could do for two days afterward was to give worship, praise, glory, and "honor and thanks to Him who sits on the throne and who lives for ever and ever" (Rev. 4:9).

Even now, I remain overwhelmed with a sense of God's love, glory, and majesty. I will never forget the glimpse God gave to me that night through the Holy Spirit.

> Praise the Lord ... who forgives all your sins and
> heals all your diseases. (Psa. 103:2-3)

Praise the Lord, indeed! Be blessed today.

33

Follow the Example of Jesus and Believe by Faith

DID YOU KNOW THAT JESUS was tempted to let His faith waiver? Did you know that Jesus was tempted to doubt God's promises? How do we know this happened? Because the Bible says it did:

> For we do not have a high priest who is unable to empathize with our weaknesses, but we have one who has been *tempted in every way, just as we are*—yet he did not sin. (Heb. 4:15, emphasis added)

So how did Jesus go about keeping His faith strong as an example for us? We know that, during His 40 long days of temptation in the wilderness, Jesus resisted temptation by quoting scriptures to Satan. Because only the Old Testament of the Bible was in existence at the time of Jesus' life on earth, here is a scripture passage from the Old Testament that Jesus could well have quoted to Satan in response to the temptation to doubt:

> I will say of the Lord, "He is my refuge and my
> fortress, my God, *in whom I will trust."*
> (Psa. 91:2, emphasis added)

Because we know for a fact that Jesus overcame doubt and unbelief, we can boldly ask for His help in doing the same ourselves. Contemplate this scripture:

> Let us then approach God's throne of grace with confidence, so that we may receive *mercy* and find *grace* to help us in our time of need.
> (Heb. 4:15, emphasis added)

Here is a suggested prayer for help:

> Father God, your only Son, Jesus, overcame doubt and unbelief when He lived as a human like me on this earth. Forgive me for my unbelief. Help me to become a person of strong, godly faith in every situation I encounter.
>
> You said in your Word that if I have faith as small as a mustard seed, You will move mountains for me. Well, Father God, I claim that promise right now in the name of Jesus. I have faith in Your Word, and I ask you to [present your request(s) here]. Thank You, Father God, for giving me my request. It is done in the name of Jesus, and I receive your blessing.

Have faith in God and His Word, my fellow believers, and *act* accordingly!

Be blessed.

34

Gift of the Holy Spirit (Part 1)

BECAUSE OF A PRONOUNCED LACK of teaching about the Holy Spirit in many churches today, it can be easy for many Christians to be confused on the subject or have unanswered questions. A common question is this: *Just what do we need the Holy Spirit for?* Here are five reasons why God wants every Christian to receive the free gift of the Holy Spirit:

1: Jesus received the Holy Spirit as an example to us.

> ... God *anointed* Jesus of Nazareth with *the Holy Spirit and power*, and ... he went around doing good and healing all who were under the power of the devil, because God was with him.
> (Acts 10:38, emphasis added)

Some of you are trying your best to work miracles and heal people without receiving God's free source of such miraculous power, the Holy Ghost.

2: "Life in the Spirit" is even more glorious than the supernatural glory that Moses experienced in the Old Testament.

Too many of us in today's modern churches want to experience God's glory in a new, higher, personal, and tangible way without accepting God's method of getting there — that is, through the power of the Holy Spirit. See 2 Corinthians 3:7-18 (please read these verses in your Bible).

3: Through the Holy Spirit, we can receive incredible power for our daily lives for our walk with God and our battle against sin, temptation, and the evil one.

This is illustrated in these passages:

> So I say, *walk by the spirit,* and you will not gratify the desires of the flesh ... Since we *live by the spirit,* let us keep in step with the spirit.
> (Gal. 5:16, 25, emphasis added)

4: The Holy Spirit is our teacher and guide.

> [Jesus said,] "But the Advocate, the Holy Spirit, whom the Father will send in my name, *will teach you all things,* and will *remind you* of everything I have said to you." (John 14:26, emphasis added)

5: God wants us to commune with Him and saturate ourselves continuously in His Holy Spirit.

> *Pray in the Spirit* on all occasions with all kinds of prayers and requests. (Eph. 6:18, emphasis added)

Do not get drunk on wine, which leads to debauchery. Instead, *be filled with the Spirit.*
(Eph. 5:18, emphasis added)

Sadly, there are more Christians who are willing to partake of earthly wine and other alcoholic spirits than are willing to be filled with God's supernatural wine, the Holy Spirit. Interestingly enough, both types of spirits are addicting, and both types can help us to accomplish things we normally wouldn't do. The choice of which spirit (or Spirit) you choose to pursue and drink from is up to you.

Be blessed today in the name of Jesus!

35

Gift of the Holy Spirit (Part 2)

THE HOLY SPIRIT HAS NINE gifts that He bestows upon us as He (the Holy Spirit) so decides to give us. Notice this scripture:

> All these [gifts] are the work of one and the same
> Spirit, and *He* distributes them to each one, just
> as *He* determines. (1 Cor. 12:11, emphasis added)

The Holy Spirit is not an "it" as referred to by some, but rather a "He." He is the third Person of the Godhead known as the Trinity, who decides which of the nine gifts each of us will receive and how these gifts will operate.

The full list of the nine gifts of the Holy Spirit can be found in 1 Corinthians 12:4-11 (please study these scripture passages in your Bible).

Of the nine gifts, there is one gift that is given by the Holy Spirit to every believer who asks for the Holy Spirit. This gift is the gift of speaking in tongues. This gift always accompanies the Holy Spirit, meaning there is no way to receive the Holy Spirit's other special gifts for us without first receiving this gift, too. The Bible says,

> [Peter and the believers with him] were aston-
> ished that the gift of the Holy Spirit had been

poured out even on Gentiles. *For they heard them speaking in tongues* and praising God …
(Acts 10:45-46, emphasis added)

So why does the Holy Spirit speak through us in a language that our minds cannot understand? Honestly, that seems to be exactly God's purpose for it; our minds all too often get in the way of what He is trying to do in us.

We know from a careful study of scripture (1 Thessalonians 5:23) that man is a *spirit* (the part of us that never dies and is either lost or saved forever), which has a *soul* (our mind, will, and emotions), and which lives in a physical *body*. Going further, prayer is our *mind* communicating with God, whereas speaking in tongues is our *spirit* communicating with God through the Holy Spirit, which bypasses our minds in the process — exactly how God designed it. Notice:

In the same way, the Spirit helps us in our weakness. *We do not know what we ought to pray for*, but the Spirit himself *intercedes* for us through wordless groans. (Rom. 8:26, emphasis added)

Because we modern Christians have the unfortunate habit of trying to understand what God wants for us before we accept or do it, the important gift of speaking in tongues is widely ignored or outright rejected in many of today's churches. To avoid speaking in tongues, many would rather reject the Holy Spirit and all of His gifts in order to escape the one gift they don't understand and don't want.

To share my experience, the Holy Spirit has given to me several distinctly different-sounding, heavenly prayer languages. One of them is what seems to be a fascinating, "symbolic" heavenly language for which there is no direct translation to any human language. In this language, sounds represent intangibles such as concepts, ideas, current and future events, relationship states, teaching points, and more.

While we cannot know all the purposes of God for blessing us with the free gift of speaking in tongues, we do know that the gift of speaking in tongues is the gateway gift to the special gifts that the Holy Spirit has uniquely offered to each of us. It's a package deal.

Be blessed today in the name of Jesus!

36

Gift of the Holy Spirit (Part 3)

TODAY WE WILL LEARN how can we can individually *choose* to receive the gift of the Holy Spirit if we want Him. To do so, first it is important to realize that receiving the gift of the Holy Spirit is an entirely separate experience from your new-birth experience as a saved Christian believer. This is clearly shown in the book of Acts:

> When [Peter and John] arrived, they prayed for the *new believers* there that they might receive the Holy Spirit, because *the Holy Spirit had not yet come on any of them*; they had simply been baptized in the name of the Lord Jesus. Then Peter and John placed their hands on them, and they received the Holy Spirit. (Acts 8:15-17, emphasis added)

Second, believe by faith that Jesus wants you and every believer to receive the Holy Spirit:

> [Jesus said] "Whoever believes in me, as scripture has said, rivers of living water will flow from within them." By this he meant the Spirit, whom those who believed in him were later to receive. Up to that time the Spirit had not been

given, since Jesus had not yet been glorified. (John 7:38-39, emphasis added)

Third, ask a believer who has already been filled with the Holy Spirit to pray with you for your own infilling of the Spirit. The believer will lay his or her hands on you in prayer, and you will receive the Holy Spirit as evidenced by speaking in a new, heavenly prayer language.

The anointing of the Holy Spirit is transferable through the laying on of hands in prayer in faith. This concept is repeatedly mentioned throughout the New Testament. One example is the passage just quoted above from the book of Acts. Here is another:

> [Paul to Timothy] Do not neglect *your gift*, which was given you through prophecy when the body of elders *laid their hands on you*. (1 Tim. 4:14, emphasis added)

When you receive the Holy Spirit, you will begin speaking in your new, heavenly prayer language. The Holy Spirit will also begin imparting additional heavenly gifts to you which will operate through you as He so desires. Along with the Spirit's other special gifts, we also receive the gift of speaking in tongues, too. Again, it is a package deal.

Those who seek the Holy Spirit will find Him. Be blessed today in the name of Jesus!

> [Jesus said,] "If you then, though you are evil, know how to give good gifts to your children, how much more will your Father in heaven give the Holy Spirit to those who ask Him! (Luke 11:13)

37

How to Increase Your Faith

HOW CAN WE INCREASE OUR FAITH? The answer is given in the Bible:

> Consequently, faith comes *from hearing* the message, and the message is *heard* through the *word about Christ.* (Rom. 10:17, emphasis added)

Notice that faith does not come by praying for more faith—after all, it takes faith to pray for faith—but rather, faith comes by *hearing* the Word about Christ.

"Hearing" the Word about Christ? Isn't "reading" the same thing? Fellow believers, let's not read scripture and then "interpret it" into what it is "supposed to mean." Instead, let's learn to take it at face value. Don't add anything to it. Simply ask, "What does the Bible say?"

Silently reading the Word of God to ourselves is what we must do when we have no other alternative. But speaking the Word of God *out loud* to ourselves is far more effective. Why?

When we speak the Word of God out loud, so much more of our brain becomes involved: first, to optically recognize and understand the words; second, to audibly pronounce the words; and a third time, when our brain's auditory circuits hear the spoken Word and process it yet again. This amplification process allows more opportunity for the Holy Spirit to work on our minds and increase our understanding and retention of the Bible.

On this note, then, here are the words of Christ, which you can read aloud to yourself today:

> [Jesus said,] "Very truly I tell you, *whoever* believes in me will do the works I have been doing, and they will do even greater things than these, because I am going to the Father. And I will do *whatever* you ask in my name, so that the Father may be glorified in the Son. You may ask me for *anything* in my name, and I will do it."
> (John 14:12-14, emphasis added)

Repeatedly, speak this aloud to yourself until you know it by heart and it becomes a part of you:

> Faith comes *from hearing* the message, and the message is *heard* through the *word about Christ*.

Be blessed today in the name of Jesus!

38

Believing the Word of God at Face Value

*[Jesus speaking] Very truly I tell you, **whoever** believes in me will do the works I have been doing, and they will do even greater things than these, because I am going to the Father ... And I will do **whatever** you ask in my name, so that the Father may be glorified in the Son. You may ask me for **anything** in my name, and **I will do it**.*

—John 14:12-14

NOW THAT YOU'VE READ the verse above, ask yourself this question: in this passage, does "whatever" and "anything" mean what it says? Or does "whatever" and "anything" really mean "some things"?

Okay, good question. What's the right answer, you ask? Answer: You decide; it's up to you. Your faith determines the practical meaning for you.

If you believe "whatever" and "anything" really mean "some things" or a "few things," then your application of this scripture is self-limited by your level of belief. If so, then for you it indeed does mean some things or a few things.

Conversely, if you believe that "whatever" and "anything" really do mean "whatever" and "anything" exactly as the scripture says, then your application of this scripture is empowered by your level of belief; so, for you it indeed does mean everything.

Here's a faith tip: Don't play out bizarre "what-if" scenarios in your head, trying to explore the boundaries of the meanings of "everything" and "whatever." Instead, simply accept this scripture for what it says at face value and move on. Stop right there; end of pondering. Don't let your mind mess up your faith.

It is a Biblical principle that our degree of belief determines what we receive from God. This was vividly illustrated by Jesus Himself while on Earth, who said it best:

> [Jesus said,] "According to your faith let it be done to you." (Matt. 9:29)

With this in mind, read this scripture:

> … If God is for us, who can be against us? He who did not spare his own Son, but gave him up for us all—*how will he not also*, along with him, *graciously give us all things*? (Rom. 8:31-32, emphasis added)

Repeatedly speak aloud John 14:12-14 to yourself (see start of this devotional) until you know it by heart and it has become a part of you. Read it aloud because "faith comes *from hearing* the message, and the message is *heard* through *the word about Christ*" (Rom. 10:17, emphasis added).

Be blessed in all you do today in the name of Jesus!

39

Don't Leave Home Without Your Shield

THE APOSTLE PAUL INSTRUCTED US to put on "the full armor of God" in Ephesians 6:10-18 so that we can "stand against the devil's schemes." Paul's description of the armor of God concludes with a final weapon, which is listed in verse 16:

> In addition to all this, take up the *shield of faith*, with which you can extinguish all the flaming arrows of the evil one. (Eph. 6:16, emphasis added)

Why is *faith* our shield? Because of the critical role our faith has in enabling the favor and blessings of God in our lives:

> And *without faith it is impossible to please God*, because anyone who comes to him must believe that he exists and that he rewards those who earnestly seek him. (Heb. 11:6, emphasis added)

This means a lack of faith isn't simply an "error" or a "missed opportunity" as can be easy for us to view it ... but rather a separating sin that blocks us from God. This is plainly stated in this scripture:

... everything that does not come from faith *is sin*. (Rom. 14:23, emphasis added)

Here are two supporting scriptures on faith:

For we *live by faith*, not by sight. (2 Cor. 5:7, emphasis added)

The only thing that counts is *faith* expressing itself through *love*. (Gal. 5:6, emphasis added)

As we saw earlier, our faith is the shield that God requires us to use to "extinguish all the flaming arrows of the evil one." Because many flaming arrows from the evil one head our way every day, our faith should be sizeable enough and in use to extinguish them.

The more we make a point of using our faith in every aspect of our daily relationship with God, the more our faith will grow. Tomorrow we will discuss in greater detail how we can grow our faith.

Don't leave home without your shield! Be blessed today in the name of Jesus.

40

Faith the Size of a Mustard Seed

THE DISCIPLES ASKED JESUS to increase their faith. Because this is a request that Christians everywhere can easily identify with, let us carefully study Jesus' answer. In reply, Jesus gave an answer that is highly revealing, although somewhat cryptic:

> The apostles said to the Lord, "Increase our faith!"
> He replied, "If you have faith as small as a mustard seed, you can say to this mulberry tree, 'Be uprooted and planted in the sea,' and it will obey you." (Luke 17:5-6)

So far, so good. Jesus then continues His reply to His disciples with a short parable about a master and his obedient servants which He summarizes as follows:

> Will [the master] thank the servant because [the servant] did what he was told to do? So you also, when you have done everything you were told to do, should say, "We are unworthy servants; we have only done our duty." (Luke 17:9-10)

,ay what? What is this supposed to mean? And what does any of Jesus' reply have to do with increasing His disciples' faith?

Answer: It really doesn't. Instead, surprisingly enough, Jesus appears to tell His disciples that their desire for more faith was both unnecessary and misplaced.

Looking closer, Jesus' complete answer not only indicates to His disciples that their existing small bit of faith was enough, but, going further, He tells them they had been thinking about things the wrong way.

Instead of viewing themselves as doing a mighty work for God, Jesus told His disciples to view themselves as merely being obedient servants who were only doing what they were told to do by their master—in this case, Jesus.

Herein is a great truth for us today. When we lay hands on the sick, we should see ourselves as merely doing what Jesus *told* us to do—not something that we want to accomplish for God or our ministry. If we see ourselves as simply doing what our Lord and Savior told us to do—nothing more or less—we will not build ourselves up as needing a lot of faith.

Jesus' answer is amazing and inspiring when viewed this way. Healing is not about what we or someone else needs; rather, it's about Jesus and what He has already done for us, what He has already given to us, and our roles as His servants in obeying Jesus simply because He told us to do it … nothing more or less. All the glory and all the attention are His … not ours. This is why a small bit of faith in God's promises in His Word is enough. We are merely servants doing our Master's bidding.

You have what is needed. Go and use your faith to set a captive of Satan free today in the name of Jesus!

41

Intercede for Our Nation

LET'S REMEMBER TO INTERCEDE in prayer for the respective countries we live in and call our home.

We know from scripture that God's judgment falls on a nation to drive it to repentance because of the sins of its rulers and its people. When God's judgment falls on a nation, everyone in that nation suffers, whether evil or righteous.

Let's review three especially striking examples of national judgment out of many such instances throughout the Bible.

First, consider the destruction of Sodom and Gomorrah in Genesis 18 and 19. The existence of just 10 righteous people in these cities would have saved them from destruction, but 10 righteous people could not be found in them, so those cites perished as a result.

Second, consider that the entire nation of Israel in Numbers 14 was condemned to wander through the desert for forty years because the majority of God's people chose to believe the evil report of ten doubting spies. This included their faithful leader, Moses, and two good spies, who were innocent and had tried their best to change the minds of the ten doubting spies. The few suffered along with the many.

Third, consider the total destruction of Jerusalem, the capital of Israel, and as many as seven million of its people who had fled there for safety from Roman Emperor Titus in 70 A.D., as foretold thirty years beforehand by Jesus:

> "Do you see all these things?" [Jesus] asked. "Truly I tell you, not one stone here will be left on another; everyone will be thrown down." (Matt. 24:2, emphasis added)

The great majority of the nation of Israel and its infrastructure was completely wiped out in this horrific national disaster because its leaders rejected and killed Jesus Christ and the apostles He sent after His death and resurrection. Again, the few righteous suffered along with the many.

In conclusion, as God's people, we should already be highly motivated by God's love overflowing in our hearts to earnestly labor and intercede for those around us who are spiritually lost and dying. However, should this motivation prove insufficient, these Biblical examples of national judgment should provide sufficient impetus.

So, let's make time to daily intercede for our respective nations and leaders from every political party who do not put God and His righteousness first in their lives. Be blessed.

42

How to Pray for Our Nation

BUILDING ON YESTERDAY'S LESSON, God's Word tells us what His people can do to turn God's anger away from an unfaithful people or nation:

> When I shut up the heavens so that there is no rain, or command locusts to devour the land or send a plague among my people, if my people, who are called by my name, will humble themselves and pray and seek my face and turn from their wicked ways, then I will hear from heaven, and I will forgive their sin and will heal their land. (2 Chron. 7:13-14)

A remarkable example of this was set by the prophet Daniel. Daniel fasted, prayed, and wept, confessing his nation's sin using first person responsibility. Specifically, Daniel confessed that *"we* have sinned" ... not *"they* have sinned." Notice carefully:

> ... *We* have sinned and done wrong. *We* have been wicked and have rebelled; *We* have turned away from your commands and laws. *We* have not listened to your servants the prophets ... We are ... covered with shame ... *We* have sinned

against you. *We* have not obeyed the Lord our
God or kept the laws he gave *us* ..."
(Dan. 9:5-6, 8, 10, emphasis added)

Daniel then asked God to intervene and save His nation
for God's sake and His great mercy ... not because His people were worthy:

> Now, our God, hear the prayers and petitions of
> your servant. For your sake, Lord, look with fa-
> vor on your [people]. We do not make requests
> of you because we are righteous, but because of
> your great mercy. Lord, listen! Lord, forgive!
> Lord, hear and act! For your sake, my God, do
> not delay, because your city and your people
> bear your name. (Dan. 9:17-19)

Remarkable. Imagine the powerful revival that would
happen if God's people, the Church, in this country all were
to pray together across this land in unity of purpose,

> Lord, we, the people of the United States, have
> sinned against You. Forgive and turn this nation
> back to You, O Lord, for Your sake and for Your
> purposes!

Amen! Let it be so in Jesus' name! Be blessed.

43

How to Pray with Confidence and Claim God's Promises

MANY CHRISTIANS PRAY WITHOUT ever specifically claiming God's promises over their situations, or they pray ineffectively out of fear of being presumptuous with God, lack of faith, or other reasons.

To strengthen our prayer life, here are examples from God's Word of how to pray effectively and claim God's promises with confidence:

> Then Jacob prayed, "O God of my father Abraham, God of my father Isaac, *Lord, you who said to me,* 'Go back to your country and your relatives, and I will make you prosper.'" (Gen. 32:9, emphasis added)

> [King David]: "And now, Lord, let the *promise* you have made concerning your servant and his house be established forever. *Do as you have promised.*" (1 Chron. 17:23, emphasis added)

> [King Solomon]: "Now Lord, the God of Israel, *keep* for your servant David my father *the promises you made to him when you said,* 'You shall

never fail to have a successor to sit before me ...'"
(1 Kings 8:25, emphasis added)

Sustain me, my God, *according to your promises,*
   and I will live; *do not let my hopes be dashed.*
   (Psa. 119:116, emphasis added)

Praying with confident faith will become natural once we realize that "God raised us up with Christ and seated us with him in the heavenly realms in Christ Jesus" (Eph. 2:6), that, in Jesus, we are "the righteousness of God" (2 Cor. 5:21), and that we are "heirs of God and co-heirs with Christ" (Rom. 8:17).

It is the evil one who would have us crawl before our Father God, begging Him for an audience. Our adversary knows this kind of weak "prayer" is not born of faith and so is ineffective.

God wants us to bring our requests before Him with confidence born out of faith, realizing who we are as the children of God. After all, God sent His Son, Jesus, to Earth as a man to make it easy for us to approach God with confidence:

> For we do not have a high priest who is unable to empathize with our weaknesses, but we have one who has been tempted in every way, just as we are—yet he did not sin. Let us then approach God's throne of grace *with confidence,* so that we may receive mercy and find grace to help us in our time of need. (Heb. 4:15-16, emphasis added)

May your faith be encouraged. Lift up your voice to our Father God in the name of His Son, Jesus, in bold confidence today!

44

Continuous Prayer
Through the Holy Spirit

SHOULD WE PRAY ALL OF THE TIME, every day, all day long?
Hmm ... Here's a better question: Given the stressful, busy
lives we all must live in this sin-sick world, is it even *possible*
for us to pray all of the time?

Answer: It indeed must be, for the Bible instructs us to
do this very thing:

Pray without ceasing. (1 Thess. 5:17, KJV,)

Here it is again, this time in the New International Version:

Pray continually. (1 Thess. 5:17)

How can we do this? Here's how. If we have the infilling of the gift of the Holy Spirit in our lives, our spirit can
indeed continuously communicate through the Holy Spirit
with our Father God. Not only this, but we can communicate with God in both directions at once. As your spirit is
praying, the Holy Spirit will continuously speak into your
spirit words of inspiration, revelation, and direction all of
the time, all throughout the day.

In fact, speaking from experience, I can share with you that continuous, bi-directional communion with God through His Holy Spirit can quickly become so natural and "normal" that, soon, you will not be able to imagine ever living your life as a Christian any other way.

This state of continuous, two-way communion is called "life in the Spirit" by Spirit-filled Christians. In turn, this continual spiritual strengthening gives us more to pray about during our times of formal prayer.

We can clearly see these two, separate, distinct prayer lives in this scripture:

> So, what shall I do? I will pray with my spirit, *but I will also pray* with my understanding; I will sing with my spirit, *but I will also sing* with my understanding. (1 Cor. 14:15, emphasis added)

Praying with our minds—termed "understanding" in the scripture above—is not possible all throughout our busy day, but continuously praying with your spirit through the Holy Spirit most certainly is. It's what God wants for us, and it's what He has asked us to do.

To learn more about the free gift of the Holy Spirit, refer to my earlier three-part series on the Holy Spirit titled, "Gift of the Holy Spirit (Parts 1 – 3)."

In conclusion, my dear fellow Believers, let us make a personal commitment now to pray without ceasing through the gift of the Holy Spirit! Be blessed today.

45

Complete Trust in
God for Everything

*[Jesus speaking] I am the vine; you are the branches.
If you remain in me and I in you, you will bear much
fruit;* **apart from me you can do nothing.**

—John 15:5

I BELIEVE THAT WHEN JESUS said in this scripture passage we
can do "nothing" He meant exactly that. Jesus was saying
that it is impossible to bear spiritual fruit without Him. We
can do *nothing* that is good or useful without Him. Jesus
wants us to choose to rely totally and completely on Him for
everything, not on our own plans and actions.

This is possible if we are experiencing continuous, two-
way communication with God through the Holy Spirit as
discussed in the previous devotional lesson in this book,
"Continuous Prayer Through the Holy Spirit." This state is
called "life in the Spirit."

Now, a huge benefit results when we choose to do nothing whatsoever apart from Jesus:

[Jesus speaking]: "*If* you remain in me and my words remain in you, *ask whatever you wish, and it will be done for you.* This is to my Father's glory, that you *bear much fruit,* showing yourselves to be my disciples." (John 15:7-8, emphasis added)

As example of this, the Holy Spirit once put it on my heart to minister to a woman waiting at an auto repair shop where I was having my wife's car fixed by her mechanic husband. While witnessing to this lady in the repair shop's small waiting area with limited seating, I noticed a tense, unfriendly-looking man come in whom I feared would sit down with us and, by doing so, disrupt my private ministry to this lady. So, I prayed in my mind through the Spirit,

Father God, in the name of Jesus, keep this man away from us until my ministry to this lady is over.

What happened? Thankfully, I was able to privately share the Word of God with this woman for over an hour while the uptight man roamed around, in and out of the shop for over an hour, but he never sat down.

The very instant I finished and quietly told the lady, "That's it. Be blessed," the man immediately came over from across the room and sat down with us. Later I related this to the woman and her mechanic husband in order to help increase their faith in God, which it did.

As noted in John 15:7-8 above, we can literally ask God for *whatever* we want in the name of His only Son, Jesus, and "It will be done for you"—that is, under the implied if not stated conditions in this scripture that we remain in Christ and Christ in us and that our purpose is to bear fruit for His Kingdom.

I believe Jesus' promise to us with all my heart, soul, mind and spirit. I pray you do likewise and that you *act* accordingly.

Go set a captive of Satan free today in the name of Jesus! Be blessed.

46

Simple Faith Like a Child Can Move Mountains

MOST OF US HAVE HEARD it said many times that Jesus wants us adults to become like little children in order to be saved. However, this commonly expressed saying is not quite what Jesus actually said. Here are Jesus' words, just as He actually spoke them:

> [Jesus said] "... the kingdom of God belongs to [little children] such as these. Truly I tell you, anyone who will not *receive* the kingdom of God like a little child will never enter it." And he took the children in his arms, placed his hands on them and blessed them. (Mark 10:14-16, emphasis added)

So, Jesus did not say that we must "be like" a little child. Rather, Jesus said that we must "receive" the kingdom of God like a little child. There's a big difference between the two.

Little children are easy to teach because they ...

1. Believe what they are told,
2. Do not question it, and
3. Immediately act upon it.

Simple faith is the trusting kind that believes simply because daddy or mommy said it and for no other reason. That's deep. Read that again. Simple faith is the exact opposite of the way most adults believe. Typically, all of our nagging questions must be answered first and our every doubt laid to rest before we will finally "believe" and then perhaps act.

But is this the kind of "faith" that God wants from us? Jesus already gave the answer to this question when He said,

> Anyone who will not *receive* the kingdom of God
> like a little child will *never* enter it.

Wow, this is awfully serious. We adults had better make sure we get this faith thing right. So, how can we adults learn to believe like little children then?

We can do so by willfully choosing daily to believe God's promises simply because our Father God said so and for no other reason, following the same example set by little children. We can daily *choose* to …

1. Believe what God says in His Word,
2. Do not question it, and
3. Immediately act upon it.

Okay … So far, so good. "I can do that," you say.

Alright, then, let's see. Here is an immediate opportunity for us to choose to suspend our intellectual understanding and choose to believe simply (and only) because Jesus said so and for no other reason:

> [Jesus said,] "You did not choose me, but I chose you and appointed you so that you might go and bear fruit—fruit that will last—and so that *whatever you ask in my name the father will give you.*" (John 15:16, emphasis added)

Whatever I ask. I personally believe Jesus' promise exactly as written here with all of my heart, soul, and mind ... not because I bother to "understand" it but simply because my Lord and Savior said it. And to no surprise at all, 100-percent true to His Word, God indeed does honor this simple faith by performing instant, on-the-spot miracles.

God wants to do for you what He has done so many times for me. I pray your faith in God's promises becomes like the simple faith of a child's, the kind of faith that moves mountains because the Word of God says it and for no other reason.

Believe in our loving Father God and His Son Jesus like a trusting little child. Go set a captive of Satan free today in the mighty name of Jesus! Be blessed.

47

Our Authority in Christ (Revisited)

THE ISRAELITES WERE TRAPPED AGAINST the Red Sea as Pharaoh and the Egyptians closed in for the kill. Naturally (or so it may seem at first), Moses cried out to God for His help.

However, notice the rebuke that God delivered to Moses in reply:

> Then the Lord said to Moses, "*Why are you crying out to me?* Tell the Israelites to move on. Raise your staff and stretch out your hand over the sea to divide the water so that the Israelites can go through the sea on dry ground." (Exod. 14:15-16, emphasis added)

Why did God say this? It was for at least three reasons.

First, the Lord had already told Moses previously, before the 10 plagues fell on Egypt, that Moses could use his staff to perform miraculous signs and wonders:

> [The Lord told Moses] "... take this staff in your hand so you can perform the signs with it." (Exod. 4:5, 17)

Second, God had also previously informed Moses that God had made Moses "like God" Himself to Pharaoh:

> Then the Lord said to Moses, "See, I have made you like God to Pharaoh ..." (Exod. 7:1)

Third, it was God Himself who, just a few days before, had told Moses to deliberately lead the Israelites into a trap against the Red Sea, specifically so God could rescue His people spectacularly and destroy the Egyptians in the process (see Exodus 14:2-4 in your Bible).

Yet, Moses managed to forget all of this and, instead, let unbelief, fear, and doubt take hold in his mind. This is why the Lord rebuked Moses, while urging him on to action.

Does this story sound familiar? It should because, all too often, this is us. Let's count the ways:

1. Like Moses' staff, God has already given to us every supernatural tool we need to defeat our enemy, the devil. (John 14:12-15; Luke 10:17-20; Mark 16:17, 18)
2. Like Moses' power over Pharaoh, God has already given to us complete power over Satan through use of the name of Jesus Christ. (Luke 10:19; Eph. 1:19-21; 2:6)
3. Like Moses, to whom God promised victory beforehand, God has likewise already promised to us victory beforehand over the evil one. (1 Cor. 15:57; 1 John 5:4)

Yet, like Moses did, the modern Christian Church today has managed to let unbelief, fear, and doubt take hold in our minds and paralyze us from defeating our enemy, despite

God's great and precious promises to us. This is why the Lord rebukes us today as He did Moses and urges us into action, just as He did with Moses long ago.

It's long past time for us to understand the mighty authority we have already been given in Christ and for us to *act* accordingly. Let each of us repent of fear and unbelief. Let us make a personal commitment to God today to not to wait any longer to *act* on our Biblical authority in Christ.

Go set a captive of Satan free today in the mighty name of Jesus! Be blessed.

48

Sacrificial Giving: God's Plan for Our Financial Success

LIKELY, ALL OF US HAVE HEARD or read the following verse many times before and undoubtedly all love hearing it:

> And my God *will meet all of your needs* according
> to the riches of his glory in Christ Jesus.
> (Phil. 4:19, emphasis added)

What a wonderful promise this is … Isn't it? Yes, it is indeed. However, notice this verse starts with the intriguing word "and." What is this word "and" referring to? To find out, let's read the previous verse. It turns out that, comparatively, few of us have ever noticed the preceding verse:

> I have received *full payment* and have more than
> enough. I am amply *supplied*, now that I have re-
> ceived from Epaphroditus *the gifts you sent*. They
> are a fragrant *offering, an acceptable sacrifice, pleas-
> ing to God*. (Phil. 4:18, emphasis added)

Then, follows that beautiful promise that we all love so much, "And my God will meet all of your needs …" that was quoted at the start.

The lesson for us: First comes our sacrificial giving …
and *then* comes God's provision of our needs.

Hmm … this puts new meaning behind this widely
quoted scripture.

In the next devotional reading, we will study an under-
appreciated story from the Bible to understand why we can
literally *give* ourselves out of a financial hole faster that we
can ever *save* or *earn* our way out. Amazing and strange to
contemplate, I know, but still true nevertheless.

Be blessed today in the name of Jesus!

49

Giving Your Way Out of a Financial Hole

BUILDING ON YESTERDAY'S DEVOTIONAL, there is a tremendous lesson we can learn from the story of Gideon in Judges 6 and 7. A massive army of enemy Midianite solders—who were "like swarms of locusts ... impossible to count" (Judges 6:5)—had invaded Israel and savagely ravaged it. Gideon's pitifully small army of 32,000 men seemed woefully insufficient to defeat them.

Gideon lacked faith in God's ability to deliver them from their horde of enemy soldiers, so he did a poor job of rallying the faith of his men. We know this for two reasons. First, Gideon's speech wasn't faith-filled but rather conveyed unbelief:

> Gideon said to God, "*If* you will save Israel by my hand as you have promised ..." (Judges 6:36, emphasis added)

Also, much like Gideon himself, his small army shook with fear in the face of the lopsided battle looming before them:

Anyone who *trembles with fear* may turn back and leave Mount Gilead … (Judges 7:3, emphasis added)

The lack of faith by Gideon and his army was not pleasing to God. We know this because God says so:

And without faith it is *impossible* to please God. (Heb. 11:6, emphasis added)

God could not bless Gideon and his army the way He wanted to in their fearful, doubting condition. So, what did God do to inspire Gideon and his army with more faith so He could then bless them with victory?

God couldn't increase the size of Gideon's army because doing so would have given them false "faith" in their strength of numbers rather than true faith in God alone so He received the glory for their victory.

So, instead, God helped increase their faith by doing exactly the opposite: God cut Gideon's already pitifully small army all the way down to just 300 men, a whopping 99-percent *decrease* in Gideon's army … *not* the big increase in his army Gideon had hoped and no doubt earnestly prayed for.

Why did God do this? By deliberately putting Gideon and his remaining 300 men into a humanly impossible situation against a vast enemy army, God put Gideon into a situation where he *had* to trust God alone for victory. It was such a crazy, lopsided losing proposition to be in that it finally dawned on Gideon once and for all that his victory was going to come from God … or that it wouldn't happen at all; period.

It worked. After Gideon overheard a dream recited by an enemy solder, Gideon boldly fired up his army with a bold declaration of faith:

> [Gideon told his men,] "Get up! *The Lord has given* the Midianite camp into your hands."
> (Judges 7:15, emphasis added)

Gideon won his victory in the supernatural with his lips before the physical battle ever started. Although Gideon had lost 99% of his army, with the remaining 1% he gained God's miraculous deliverance in return for his faith.

Interestingly enough, the story of Gideon applies directly to our finances today. Our natural tendency, when trapped in a financial hole, is to try to *save* or *earn* our way out. However, this typically gives us false "faith" in our own actions instead of true faith in God and God alone.

Instead, in order to climb out of a financial hole, we should *give* our way out.

When we are short on funds but nevertheless radically give beyond and above our tithe, we put ourselves into a position where we have no other financial alternative for saving ourselves. When it's either God or nothing, the stage is finally set for us to trust God and God alone radically for our deliverance. This type of faith allows God to work miraculous wonders on our behalf.

As a result of three miraculous experiences in my finances during a two-month period of great loss and uncertainty, I can share with you my personal testimony that giving until there nothing else left whatsoever to rely on but God is a terrific way to climb out of a serious financial crisis.

That's because God is *always* faithful to His Word, and He *always* miraculously honors our bold faith in His promises.

God provides, but we must be faithful and diligent in doing our share. Then He steps in at our point of weakness as we rely on Him in faith.

Be blessed today in the name of Jesus!

50

Handling Financial Difficulty by Faith

[Jesus speaking] I chose you and appointed you so that you might go and bear fruit—fruit that will last—and so that whatever you ask in my name the Father will give you.

—John 15:16

*[Jesus speaking] Therefore I tell you, **do not worry about your life**, what you will eat or drink; or about your body, what you will wear. Is not life more than food, and the body more than clothes? [...] Therefore do not worry about tomorrow, for tomorrow will worry about itself. Each day has enough trouble of its own.*

—Matthew 6:25, 34

MANY BELIEVERS IN CHRIST—including myself—for years have refused to follow the words of Jesus exactly as written in these two verses. So often we will not ask and rest in faith, but instead we worry about both today and tomorrow. As a result, we do not receive, and then our lack of belief is proven correct as we see it.

However, during a time of severe financial crisis in my life, I finally chose for the first time to let go of my control of my financial future. Instead, I began to choose daily to walk by faith, trusting God completely for His provision rather than in my own wisdom, stressful effort, and planning.

The difference was like night and day. When I do it through my own efforts, it's just a piece of bread. When God does it, it's a piece of bread that has been multiplied into a multitude fed … with twelve baskets of leftovers!

I had been unemployed during those two months while working to build a new information security consulting business from scratch … without any financial assets, reserves, or income of any kind. However, each day, I would get up and speak God's promises over my finances for that day, while believing that my needs for that day would be met through God's providence alone. My wife, Michelle, was totally united with me in faith in this effort. Each day, God miraculously provided the resources needed to purchase everything necessary to build my new business and feed my family along the way.

For two months, God continued to provide for us each day from sources and methods out of the blue, exactly when needed and not a day sooner. God's timing amazed me beyond belief.

Then, my brand-new consulting company won its first job … from a company we did not contact and had only recently found out about us. They approached us out of the blue on a Friday night. They asked for no references and no insurance or bonding—thankfully, because we did not yet have insurance. Nevertheless, amazingly enough they signed our short statement of work without asking for a proposal or negotiating a discount off our full consulting rates. They even agreed without negotiation or comment to pay us a large retainer payment up front. They did this, thankfully, without first performing a corporate credit check as per usual. (That was a good thing because my company was brand new and, therefore, had no corporate credit!)

The job was a very lucrative, significant win for us that I never saw coming.

In utter amazement, all I could do was ask myself, "How did we win this job?" I knew the answer then, and so do you now: it resulted from the divine favor and miraculous blessing of our dear Father God Himself ... and for this reason only and nothing more. Nothing we did won that job. God alone gets all the glory. Thank you, dear Father God!

God wants to do for you what He did for me. "Do not worry about tomorrow," Jesus said. We must learn to trust God completely and only *by faith* in His promises for His blessings, one day at a time and not in our own wisdom and efforts. Be blessed today in the name of Jesus!

51

Putting God First in Our Day

HOW DO YOU START YOUR DAY? Do you jump out of bed, rush out the door, and barely make it to work on time? Do you faithfully watch the morning news or shows on TV? Do you eat breakfast? Do you hit the gym for some exercise? Do you worship, study your Bible, and pray?

For that matter, does it even really matter how we start our day? If our hearts are right and our intentions are pure, does it honestly even matter when we study our Bibles or pray during our day?

In response, let's see what the Word of God has to say on the subject of timing:

> Very early in the morning, while it was still dark, Jesus got up, left the house and went off to a solitary place, *where He prayed*. (Mark 1:35, emphasis added)

> I rise *before dawn* and *cry for help*;
> I have put my hope *in your word*.
> (Psa. 119:147, emphasis added)

Hear my cry for help, my King and my God, for
to you I pray.
In the morning, Lord, you hear my voice; *in the
morning* I lay my requests before you and
wait expectantly. (Psa. 5:2-3, emphasis added)

... *Morning by morning* [the Lord] dispenses his
justice, and *every new day* he does not fail ...
(Zeph. 3:5, emphasis added)

Then Moses said to them, "No one is to keep any
of it until morning." However, some of them
paid no attention to Moses; they kept part of it
until morning, but it was full of maggots and began to smell. So Moses was angry with them.
(Exod. 16:19-20)

Looking at this last scripture, we see that yesterday's
manna (God's blessings) is not good for today; instead, God
wants us to collect new manna from Him every morning.

But *first* in our day? Yes. From the following scripture,
we see that God's special manna for us today will vanish if
we wait until later in the day. Read for yourself:

Each morning everyone gathered as much as they
needed, and *when the sun grew hot, it melted away.*
(Exod. 16:21, emphasis added)

Snooze and we lose. There should be no surprise here.
God wants to be first in our lives, in our money, in our day,
and in everything we do. Consider the words of Jesus, who
lived on this earth as a man as our example:

[Jesus said,] "But seek *first* his kingdom and his righteousness, and all these things (that we need) will be given to you as well." (Matt. 6:33, emphasis added)

How great is our need of God, His righteousness, and His blessings?

For my part, every day of the week, I choose to believe that seeking God "first" in my day means exactly that: "first" … not later on in my day when I have more time or when it may be more convenient.

Think of the honor we show God when our *first* food and drink of our day is God's Word and His sweet Holy Spirit … rather than earthly food and drink.

If you aren't doing so already, I pray that you will make the decision today to pursue God *first* in your day, every day. Over time, you will be blessed more than you can know right now because of the decision you made today.

(For additional tips and pointers about how we should start our day, every day, see the devotional lesson in this book titled, "Zeal for God and His Kingdom.")

52

The Greatest Commandment in Action

[Jesus speaking] A new command I give you: Love one another. As I have loved you, so you must love one another.

—John 13:34

And now these three remain: faith, hope and love. But the greatest of these is love.

—1 Cor. 13:13

HOW SHOULD WE LOVE our fellow mankind? Here are two scriptures that provide the answer:

> The only thing that counts is faith expressing itself through love. (Gal. 5:6b)

> In the same way, faith by itself, if it is not accompanied by action, is dead. (Jam. 2:17)

Notice that God does not want from us love without faith, faith without love, or love without action. Rather, what God wants from us is *love in action through faith*. God is well pleased when all three of these attributes work together harmoniously in our lives to bear fruit for His kingdom.

There are many ways we can demonstrate our love for others. Using our faith to pray for healing of the sick is just one of many powerful ways we can allow God to use us to show our love.

Find someone to love in action through faith today! Be blessed in Jesus' name.

53

Confidence Before God

WE HAVE A SPECIAL LESSON TODAY that I hope you will remember for the rest of your natural life here on earth which will bless you wherever you go and in whatever you do.

First, we begin with an important scripture passage of which we should take note and read carefully:

> This is how we *know* that we belong to the truth and how we set our hearts *at rest* in his presence … *If our hearts do not condemn us*, we have *confidence* before God and receive from him *anything* we ask, because we keep his commands and do what pleases him. And this is his command: to believe in the name of his Son, Jesus Christ, and to love one another as he commanded us. The one who keeps God's commands lives in him, and he in them. And this is how we *know* that he lives in us: We know it by the spirit he gave us. (1 John 3:19-24, emphasis added)

These verses are hugely important because they directly impact our ability—and even our desire—to minister to others in faith for the things they need, including for their instant, miraculous healing.

This is important because of the insidious way that Satan tempts our minds whenever we begin to minister to someone for their healing. We've all had it happen. The devil will whisper the following lies to us:

"You are not worthy." (Right ... and we never will be worthy either, except for the blood of Jesus covering us which makes us perfect in God's sight. See Hebrews 4:15-16).

"There is sin in your life." (Right again. While God does not honor the prayers of those who cherish willful, known sin in their lives, the one-time sacrifice of Jesus is our atonement if we have accepted His righteousness by faith. See 2 Corinthians 5:19).

"God isn't listening to your prayer. You are wasting your time. A miracle isn't going to happen. You are way out on a limb on your own on this one, Buddy Boy." (Oh really? The scriptures just quoted above allow us to deal decisively with the temptation to doubt). Here's a repeat of that crucial, final verse:

> And this is how we *know* that he lives in us: We know it by the Spirit he gave us. (1 John 3:24b, emphasis added)

When the temptation to doubt comes from the evil one, a highly effective, powerful response I have discovered is praying aloud in tongues, "the language of angels" (1 Cor. 13:1). Praying aloud in tongues through the Holy Ghost is an immediate testimony to both my spirit and to Satan that God's sweet Spirit is in and with me. Prayer through the Holy Spirit is an extremely reassuring and comforting blessing from God that those without it cannot know.

When I am ministering to the sick in the presence of those who I can tell either do not believe in speaking in tongues or who are not comfortable with it, I typically pray in the Spirit in a barely audible whisper. However, when I am ministering among those who have the Gift of the Holy Spirit, I pray in the Spirit out loud.

As I hear the audible outpouring of the Holy Spirit from the lips of those around me, my faith is increased still further, and their faith in turn is increased by hearing me. As our mutual faith rises higher and higher, the power of the Holy Spirit continually intensifies. God responds with an outpouring of mighty miracles, signs, and wonders just as He did for the early Church in the *Book of Acts*. Do not be surprised at this, my friends. After all, we know from scripture that "Jesus Christ is the same yesterday and today and forever" (Heb. 13:8).

One more time:

We know it by the Spirit he gave us.
(1 John 3:24b)

Opening your mouth and letting the Holy Spirit pour through becomes an instant testimony and a witness both to yourself and to the tempting, listening evil spirits that God is with you and is listening to your prayer (see also 2 Cor. 5:5). Your faith rises, and on the spot, God performs the miracle you have been seeking.

God does not ask you to attempt first to understand how or why His Spirit works, or for all the reasons why speaking in tongues is beneficial, before He gives His free gift of the Holy Ghost. The Holy Spirit cannot be intellectually understood. Instead, He can only be *experienced*. God designed it this way for our own good. You must trust God first and then, by faith, believe God promises and put God's Word into action in our lives. You will then begin to experience the deep things of the Holy Spirit … but never beforehand.

God bless you. Through the power of the Holy Spirit, I urge you to go set a captive of satan free today in the mighty name of Jesus! Be blessed.

54

Love One Another
As Christ Loves Us

*[Jesus speaking]: "A new command I give you: **love one another**. As I have loved you, so you must love one another. By this everyone will know that you are my disciples, **if you love one another**."*

—John 13:34-35

JESUS AND HIS DISCIPLES THROUGHOUT the New Testament of the Bible repeatedly instruct us to "love one another." But what exactly does this mean? Are we sure we know what is being asked of us?

Let's dig deeper. From 1 Corinthians 13:4-8, we learn the attributes of godly love. Namely, love is ...

- Patient
- Kind
- Unselfish
- Humble
- Trusting
- Protecting
- Reliable (does not fail)

Finally, one more important attribute is listed:

- Keeps no record of wrongs

Ouch! This means keeping my injury counter on zero ... all of the time.

I know I don't do this as consistently as I should. If I did, then every time someone hurt or offended me in some way, I would regard it as being their very first time to do so. How in the world am I going to do this? By His grace, of course. While this is not easy for us to do because of our sinful natures, God clearly wants us to do just this very thing.

Just think ... It is much easier for us to forgive our spouses, children, co-workers, boss, others, etc. when we are hurt by their first offenses against us ... than it is to forgive them for their 10th offense in the last day or month.

So, what would happen if we stopped keeping score? What if, each time someone slighted or hurt us in some way, we regarded it as their very first offense against us rather than their 99th? Not keeping score anymore changes everything!

> Above all, love each other *deeply*, because *love covers over a multitude of sins.* (1 Pet. 4:8, emphasis added)

Let's reset our hurt counters to zero today. Go love on someone you've had difficulties with in the name of Jesus!

55

The Incredible, One-Time Sacrifice of Jesus

MY PRECIOUS, COVENANT, WIFE-FOR-LIFE and ministry partner, Michelle, was listening to her YouVersion Bible app on her smartphone the other night, which was reading aloud the Old Testament sacrifice rituals from the books of Leviticus and Numbers. As chapter after chapter of tedious detail about endless sacrificial routine went by, one thing became very clear.

Michelle and I agreed that every believer in Christ should carefully read Leviticus and Numbers in order to fully appreciate the enormity of the perfect, one-time sacrifice for all time made for us by our Lord and Savior, Jesus Christ.

Although quoting only a tiny excerpt here from these two lengthy books cannot compare with reading them completely in meticulous detail as just described, nevertheless, here we can get a minuscule glimpse of the level of ritual sacrifice that God required in order to atone for sin under the Old Covenant:

> [God's instructions to the Israelites]: ...offer a
> burnt offering of one young bull, one ram and
> seven male lambs a year old, *all without defect.*

With the bull offer a grain offering ... Include one male goat as a sin offering ... These are *in addition to* the monthly and daily burnt offerings with their grain offerings and drink offerings as specified. They are food offerings presented to the Lord, a pleasing aroma. (Num. 29:2-6, emphasis added)

The writer of Hebrews summarized the entire sacrifice ritual of the Old Covenant as follows:

Day after day every priest stands and performs his religious duties; *again and again* he offers the same sacrifices, *which can never take away sins.* (Heb. 10:11, emphasis added)

In stark contrast, compare the Old Testament's mind-numbing sacrificial ritual with the incredible, one-time sacrifice for our sins made by God's only Son, Jesus Christ, that we may have eternal life with Him in the world to come:

But when this priest [Jesus] had offered *for all time one sacrifice for sins,* he sat down at the right hand of God, and since that time he waits for his enemies to be made his footstool. For by *one sacrifice* he has made perfect *forever* those who are being made holy. (Heb. 10:12-14, emphasis added)

The continuous slaughter of millions of spotless, blameless animals every year for over a thousand years under the Old Testament could not in sum total accomplish what the one-time sacrifice of Jesus Christ was able to do—that is, achieve the permanent forgiveness of sins for all those who make Jesus the Lord and Savior of their lives. A one-time sacrifice that is good for all of mankind everywhere ... *forever*! And without us having to do a thing other than accept it! I find the contrast of what Jesus has done for us to be simply mind-boggling to contemplate in its scope of magnitude, accomplishment, and implications.

If you haven't already done so today, fall on your knees, and thank God our Father for the ultimate sacrifice for all time made by His Son, Jesus, for us so that we might have eternal escape from the penalty for our sins and live with Him forever.

Prayer Starter: "Thank You, Jesus! I renew my commitment to serve You as Lord and Savior of my life. I will gladly share the Good News about You with others so they can be saved from the coming destruction ... just as You saved me. I love You, Jesus, and I will show it with my actions by obeying Your command to tell others what You have done for me!"

Be blessed today in the name of Jesus!

56

Jesus, Friend of
Sinners and the Abused

THINK FAST. HERE'S A Bible trivia question that you can ask your friends today ... after you first solve it yourself, of course. Here goes:

What do a sexual abuse victim, a heathen prostitute, and a cold-blooded murderer have in common in the Bible?

Do you give up?

Answer: All three people are part of the ancestry lineage of Jesus. Hard to believe?

Let's take a close look at Matthew 1, which documents "the genealogy of Jesus the Messiah" (Matt: 1:1). In Jesus' family lineage listed in this chapter, we see a number of characters with a tainted or soiled past. Here are three who I personally find the most interesting:

Verse 3: "Judah the father of Perez and Zerah, whose mother was Tamar ..."

Who was Tamar? Tamar's husband died, and she was subsequently sexually taken advantage of by her father-in-law, Judah. Then, even worse yet, she was nearly burned to death for being the victim (see Tamar's story in Genesis 38). Despite her troubles, Tamar is part of the lineage of Jesus.

Verse 5a: "Salmon the father of Boaz, whose mother was Rahab ... "

Who was Rahab? Rahab not only was a prostitute, she was a foreign, heathen prostitute at that. Yet, Rahab is part of the lineage of Jesus also. More on Rabab shortly.

Verse 6: 'David was the father of Solomon, whose mother had been Uriah's wife ... "

Who was David? David committed adultery and then committed first-degree, cold-blooded murder in an attempt to cover up his adultery (see 2 Samuel 11). Yet David forms a key part of the lineage of Jesus. God even called David "a man after my own heart" (Acts 13:22).

Going back to Rahab the prostitute, the Bible even calls her "righteous":

> In the same way, was not even Rahab the prostitute *considered righteous* for what she did when she gave lodging to the spies and sent them off in a different direction? (Jam. 2:25, emphasis added; see Joshua 2-6 for the story of Rabab)

There you have it. Jesus truly was and is the ultimate "friend of sinners" (Matt. 11:19) ... so much so that it is apparent from Jesus' family lineage that His love and acceptance of sinners started long before He was even born.

The son of extremely poor parents, Jesus was born in a bed of hay in an animal pen. Why? Because Jesus was poor so we can be rich (2 Cor. 8:9). Because Jesus made Himself absolutely nothing, we can have everything. This conundrum is stated best by the Apostle Paul:

> [Jesus] made himself *nothing* by taking the very nature of a servant, being made in human likeness. And being found in appearance as a man, he *humbled himself* by becoming obedient to *death*—even death on a cross! *Therefore* God exalted him to the *highest place* and gave him the name that is above every name, that at the name of Jesus every knee should bow, in heaven and on earth and under the earth, and every tongue acknowledge that Jesus Christ is Lord, to the glory of God the Father. (Phil. 2:7-11, emphasis added)

I don't know about you, but my heart has been captivated once again by this humble Man who created us in the first place and then chose to humble Himself even unto death in order to win us back ... not by force but through His perfect love. How utterly amazing!

Truly, Jesus deserves His exalted position in Heaven and Earth as "King of Kings and Lord of Lords" (Rev. 19:16).

Worship our God and Savior Jesus with all of your heart, soul, and mind today (Luke 10:25-28)! Be blessed.

57

Faith vs. Feelings: What to Do When Things Don't Feel Right

RECENTLY, I HAD ONE of those strange days that happens from time to time where my day just didn't feel right. I woke up feeling lost and disconnected from God. I just didn't feel holy, special, and beloved of God like all members of God's Church here on Earth are.

In fact, although I was not aware of anything I had done that should make me feel this way, I still felt as if I had somehow messed up and separated myself from the love of Christ.

Have you ever experienced a day like this? Most Christians have or will at some point in their walk with God. Either way, I want to share with you how the Lord helped me to get through this experience.

First of all, the Holy Spirit reminded me that my salvation is based on my *faith,* not on my *feelings.* Whereas my feelings can be affected by my circumstances and influenced by the evil one, instead through it all, I must choose to trust God and His promises in His Word.

It occurred to me that, if I allowed my feelings rather than my faith to guide my day, I soon would have a problem that actually *would* cause an issue between God and me. So, I chose to turn to God's Word, where I found this:

> Therefore, brothers and sisters, since we have *confidence* to enter the Most Holy Place by the blood of Jesus ... let us draw near to God with a sincere heart and with *the full assurance that faith brings*, having our hearts sprinkled *to cleanse us from a guilty conscience* and having our bodies washed with pure water. (Heb. 10:19, 22; emphasis added)

There it is again ... the critical role of faith in our daily walk with God.

> And without faith it is *impossible* to please God. (Heb. 11:1, emphasis added)

I made a decision right then to believe God's promises rather than my feelings. I decided to choose to have a good day, trusting in the Lord, and I did.

Not only that, I went on the offensive against Satan, rebuking him out loud in the name of Jesus for even trying to get me to believe his lies. This may be too radical for some, I know, but all I can tell you is that this spoken act of bold faith allowed the power of God to put Satan to flight and to rectify my situation immediately.

Spiritual warfare is real! Don't take the temptations of the devil by lying down in weakness. Instead, get up and boldly fight back by using the mighty name of Jesus!

Be blessed today in the Lord.

58

Don't Let Satan Rob Your Worthiness Before God

OUR FAITH WILL FALTER WHEN we do not realize our worthiness before God through our Lord Jesus Christ. And when our faith falters, we either will not ask God at all for the miraculous, or if we do, our prayers will go unanswered. So, let's study of the Word of God on this subject, this time using the God's Word Translation of the Bible simply because this translation focuses on reverent simplicity of understanding. Read carefully:

> God has *rescued us* from the power of darkness and has brought us into the kingdom of his Son, whom he loves. His Son paid the price to free us, which means that our sins are *forgiven*. ... But now Christ has brought you back to God by dying in his physical body. He did this so that you could come into God's presence *without sin, fault, or blame*. This is on the *condition* that you continue in *faith* without being moved from the solid foundation of the hope that the Good News contains. (Col. 1:13-14, 22-23 GWT, emphasis added)

Now, here is the same passage again, this time in the more accurate, yet-still-readability-focused New International Version (NIV):

> But now [God] has reconciled you by Christ's physical body through death to present you *holy* in his sight, *without blemish and free from accusation—if* you continue in your *faith*, established and *firm*, and *do not move* from the hope held out in the gospel. (Col. 1:22-23, emphasis added)

And here is another scripture on this important subject:

> Who will bring any charge against those whom God has chosen? It is God who justifies. Who then is the one who condemns? *No one.* Christ Jesus who died—more than that, who was raised to life—is at the right hand of God and is also interceding for us. (Rom. 8:33-34, emphasis added)

Before we go any further, let me say right now that this discussion isn't meant to be any kind of a "license to sin." Those who are looking for a way to justify their evil desires and actions will always find a way to do so. This message isn't intended for such individuals.

Rather, it is meant for those believers who are sincerely striving to be pure and holy before God, but constantly let themselves slip back into a feeling of unworthiness before God. This feeling robs these believers of their faith and prevents the type of effective, faith-filled prayer that gets results. As a result, God is limited in His ability to perform the miraculous on their behalf.

Each of us must choose daily to accept Christ's white robe around us so that we can come "with *confidence* before the throne of grace" (Heb. 4:16), presenting our requests in faith and full assurance. Every day, each of us must settle in our hearts that the Word of God is true for each of us, individually and uniquely, not just for others that we may "feel" are somehow holier or more worthy than we are. None of us ever are or ever will be worthy, except through our acceptance of the covering blood of Jesus alone.

Once we understand that it is Christ's righteousness that makes us worthy, rather than anything we have done or can ever do, our faith will be strong and firm and will allow God to respond to our prayers with the miraculous.

Put on the white robe of Jesus today! Allow His worthiness before God to cover you today. More on this subject tomorrow.

Be blessed in the name of Jesus!

59

Put on the
Righteousness of Jesus

JESUS TOLD OF A GREAT KING who prepared a great wedding banquet but whose invited guests made excuses and did not come. Jesus was no doubt referring not only to God's people, the Jews of His day who rejected Jesus, but also to all those throughout time who would reject Him as well. Jesus told what the king did next:

> Then [the king] said to his servants, "The wedding banquet is ready, but those I invited did not deserve to come. So go to the street corners and invite to the banquet *anyone* you find." So the servants went out into the streets and gathered *all* the people they could find, *the bad as well as the good*, and the wedding hall was filled with guests. (Matt. 22:8-10, emphasis added)

So far, so good. Now, notice what happened next:

> But when the king came in to see the guests, he noticed a man there who was *not wearing wedding clothes*. He asked, "How did you get in here without wedding clothes, friend?" The man was

speechless. Then the king told the attendants, "Tie him hand and foot, and throw him outside, into the darkness ... " (Matt. 22:11-12, emphasis added)

Verse 10 (above) gives us a clue of how this happened: the guests who were brought in included "the bad as well as the good" people. So, I surmise that a guest came in who didn't "feel" worthy. Therefore, this guest either never put on the wedding clothes that were given to everyone, or put them on initially but then took them back off out of a sense of "feeling" unworthy.

Instead of this guest wearing his wedding garments and believing he was worthy because the king said he was worthy, this guest chose to listen to a lie of the enemy that he was not worthy. Therefore, he refused to put on or removed Christ's robe of righteousness from himself.

The key takeaway thought to remember from this parable is that it is God's perception of us that matters ... not our own perception of ourselves.

One more time:

But now [God] has reconciled you by Christ's physical body through death to present you *holy* in his sight, *without blemish and free from accusation*—**if** you continue in your *faith*, established and *firm*, and *do not move* from the hope held out in the gospel... (Col. 1:22-23, emphasis added)

Also, one more time, here is a repeat warning from yesterday's devotional lesson: This discussion isn't meant to be any type of a "license to sin." Those who are looking for a way to justify their evil thoughts, desires, and actions will always find a way to do so … despite the fact that the Bible is abundantly clear that we must confess, repent, overcome, and turn away from our sins and live in victory.

The past three devotionals were written for those who are genuinely striving to overcome but allow a sense of their own unworthiness to undermine how God views them—that is, pure, holy, and righteous in His sight. All God sees is His Son's righteousness around us that makes us worthy, provided that we accept Christ's sacrifice for us and don't take off His white robe from around us.

Once we fully understand and, more importantly, *act* on the fact that it is Christ's righteousness that makes us worthy rather than anything we have ever done or can ever do, our faith and confidence before God (Heb. 4:16) will allow Him to respond to our prayers with the miraculous, including signs and wonders.

Put on the white robe of Jesus today and keep it on! Allow His worthiness before God to cover you today. You are worthy because Jesus is worthy! Incredible, but true. Praise God for His wondrous and amazing plan of salvation! Be blessed today in the name of Jesus.

60

Overcoming Sin and Temptation (Part 1)

YES, IT IS TRUE THAT WE Christian believers have sinful human natures (Romans 8). Yes, it is true that we are stuck with our sinful human natures until Jesus returns to this earth to transform us into our new bodies and holy natures.

However, this doesn't mean we can't do a much better job of overcoming sin and temptation in the meantime until Jesus returns. The battle to overcome more effectively starts with what we pray for and seek from God. After all, as we know from prior devotional lessons in this book, Jesus said, "According to your faith let it be done to you" (Matt. 9:29).

Overcoming sin is the same as with physical healing; we receive from God what we believe and ask God for in the name of His Son, Jesus Christ, and act on by faith.

If we do not believe we can overcome, we will not ask God to overcome, using the type of faith that moves mountains. And if we fail to ask God in faith, we will not receive what we ask for. And if we receive the power we need but then fail to act on it, it will not manifest.

For the same reason, miraculous physical healing manifests when we act on it *first* before we see the miracle, according to the words of Jesus (Mark 11:24—also see prior devotionals in this book for a thorough review of this subject).

Can overcoming really be this "simple"? Yes, it really is this straightforward, although I would not say it is always easy to do.

Overcoming is critically important to the exercise of our faith because it is our faith that enables God to respond with the miraculous on our behalf. We see this principle in this scripture:

> [We] receive from him *anything* we ask, because *we keep his commands* and *do what pleases him.*
> (1 John 3:22, emphasis added)

God will not respond to us with the miraculous if we are not doing what He asked us to do (see also John 15:7).

So, to kick off this three-part series on *overcoming*, let's start from the beginning:

> For we do not have a high priest who is unable to *empathize* with our weaknesses, but we have one who has been *tempted* in every way, just as we are—yet he did not sin. Let us then approach God's throne of grace with confidence, so that we may receive *mercy* and find *grace to help us* in our time of need. (Heb. 4:15-16, emphasis added)

Let's be honest with ourselves; this scripture is only nice-to-know information unless we understand and apply it to our daily lives. So, here are several key points in this scripture to take special note of ...

Temptation should not be equated as being sin. The devil will often try to convince us that we have sinned when we are seriously tempted ... in order to convince us that we have failed and can't beat the temptation. This paves the way for us to give in to sin for real.

Temptation can produce real suffering, which shouldn't be regarded as failure or something a "good believer" wouldn't go through unless something was wrong with him or her.

Jesus truly understands and sympathizes with our sufferings when we are under temptation because He suffered temptation as a man here on Earth exactly as we suffer.

Jesus wants to empathize with us and cover us with His grace and mercy while still helping us to overcome and turn away from our sins ... if we will approach Him with confidence and *expectation* in this regard.

Think about this scripture, meditate on it and pray about it. Looking at things this way, ask yourself what you should do differently the next time you are tempted. Ask the Holy Spirit to reveal the right answers to you.

Be blessed today in the name of Jesus!

61

Overcoming Sin and Temptation (Part 2)

LET'S BEGIN PART 2 OF THIS SERIES with a question: Is Satan to blame when we are tempted with sin?

Certainly, we can point the finger of blame at Satan if we wish, but according to the Word of God, we really should point it at ourselves. Take a look at this revealing scripture from the Apostle James, the half-brother of Jesus:

> When tempted, no one should say, "God is tempting me." For God cannot be tempted by evil, nor does he tempt anyone; but each person is tempted when they are dragged away *by their own evil desire* and enticed. (Jam. 1:13-14, emphasis added)

In other words, Satan doesn't cause our evil desires. He merely *appeals* to our evil desires that he observes we are vulnerable to or are already struggling with. Read that again.

So, can we do anything to lessen the evil desires of our sinful human natures within us? Absolutely. We can do a lot. Here are two scriptures on this important topic:

I have *hidden your word in my heart*
that I might not sin against you.
(Psa. 119:11, emphasis added)

Do not conform to the pattern of this world, but
be transformed by the renewing of your mind. Then
you will be able to test and approve what God's
will is—his good, pleasing and perfect will.
(Rom. 12:2, emphasis added)

So, is transforming our minds through the Word of God
the way to overcome?

Yes, that's an important part of the answer for sure.
However, some of you aren't going to like me anymore after
I tell you the rest of it.

Here it is ... What good does studying the Word of God
do if we pollute our minds faster than the Word of God can
transform our minds? How can 5 or maybe 30 minutes of
Bible study a day outweigh the average of 5 hours of television and cable programs that the average American watches
each day?

Answer: It doesn't. Our minds will remain just as polluted as before and our faith just as challenged as before.

So, what's the answer, then? My family and I may occasionally watch a carefully selected good family movie together once a week via DVD/Blu-ray or streaming media
when my wife is sitting right next to me, just in case, to help
me protect my eyes, the gateway to my mind.

But in our home, always-on TV or cable with its highly
variable content and surprise commercials is not an option
for us. The inappropriate dress, saucy images, unending
sexual innuendo, trashy commercials, and huge waste of

valuable time are too much, so we don't watch TV or have a cable subscription.

And during my frequent business trips, I do not watch TV then either. I have not turned the TV on in my hotel rooms since September 2011, shortly after starting Bible college. Instead, I play praise and worship music in my room, pray, study the Bible, and play worship music.

Some of you are thinking, "Wow, Paul, this is radical. You really must have a problem with lust." Actually no, it's the other way around: I don't have a problem with lust because I take radical preemptive action against it.

In my experience with myself and through our marriage counseling ministry with others, I believe that 80 percent of the battle with lust that the average male Christian believer needlessly puts himself through originates from what he watches on TV. The problem starts there and kicks off a cycle of temptation elsewhere. In turn, the temptation to lust is perpetually kept alive by still more TV.

For many Christian women, reading saucy romance novels, watching soap operas on TV, and flirting have the same cause-and-effect results.

While lust isn't the only sin we have to overcome, it is one of the hardest for many, so I am merely using it as an example of the successful, overcoming thought process. My dear friends, we *can* overcome temptation and sin. Check it out for yourself:

> Religion that God our Father accepts as pure and faultless is this: to look after orphans and widows in their distress and to *keep oneself* from being *polluted by the world.* (Jam. 1:27, emphasis added)

We *can* keep our minds from being polluted by the world. Turning off Satan's perpetually running, one-eyed monster (the TV) in our own homes is a large start toward doing just that. As just mentioned, that's perhaps 80 percent of the battle toward conquering one of our biggest major temptations right there.

Be blessed today in the mighty name of Jesus!

62

Overcoming Sin and Temptation (Part 3)

*Make **every effort** to live in peace with everyone **and to be holy**; without holiness no one will see the Lord.*

—Hebrews 12:14

IT IS WORTH REALIZING THAT some of our biggest struggles with sin result not from current events, but rather as a result of our memories from our past failures and sins. All of us have done sinful things in the past. Memories of these past "pleasures" of sin may suddenly come flooding to the forefront of our consciousness at the worst possible times and, therefore, become unexpected and powerful sources of temptation to sin from within us.

True enough. So, what, if anything, can we do about stopping such impure memories?

Purging Impure Memories

I can only share with you what God has done for me. After years of attempting to deal with polluted memories going around and around in my head, several years ago I asked God to remove these sinful memories from my mind. I prayed,

> Father God, you created me, and you can do anything You want. You promised in your Word to do anything I ask you to do in the name of your Son, Jesus. Father God, remove those sinful memories (details here) so that they are permanently gone for good from my mind and never ever trouble me again.

On the spot, God immediately answered my prayer. I found that, even if I tried, I could no longer recall the sinful images that had troubled me so much for many years. While I could still remember that I had sinned in general, all of the sinful imagery had abruptly vanished from my mind. Now, years later, it's still the same; no matter how hard I try, I simply cannot recall those poisonous images and memories anymore. They are gone for good. Praise God on high!

Anything Means Anything

Some of you may be surprised that God would do something like this. Really? Should you be surprised? What does the Bible have to say on the subject? Read for yourself:

> [Jesus speaking] I will do *whatever* you ask in my name, so that the Father may be glorified in the Son. You may ask me for *anything* in my name, *and I will do it.* (John 14:12-14, emphasis added)

I simply choose every day to believe that "whatever" and "anything" means exactly what Jesus said. Do you? Your degree of belief in the words of life spoken by Jesus will determine what you will receive from God. This principle was vividly illustrated by Jesus Himself while on earth:

> [Jesus said,] "According to your faith let it be done to you." (Matt. 9:29)

What we believe is what we will receive from God. If you will not believe it, you will not receive it. It's that simple. Nowhere is the term *self-fulfilling prophecy* more applicable than to what we choose to believe God for.

Breaking Demonic Strongholds

What's next? What else, you ask, can we pray for in our battle against sin?

Answer: We can ask our Father God to break the power of binding addictions over our lives.

As an example, as part of a weekly church ministry outreach to the homeless in downtown Houston, an obviously inebriated, unsteady-on-his-feet homeless man asked me to pray for him. He explained that he had tried to stop drinking for many years, but had always slipped back and been unable to stay sober. He said he desperately wanted to quit once and for all.

In response, I led him in praying the following prayer:

> Father God, I repent for harming my body. Forgive me in Jesus' name. I am trapped by my sin, and I need your supernatural help to escape.

Next, I spoke directly to the evil spirit responsible for the demonic stronghold over the drunk man's life:

> You evil spirit of addiction, in the name of Jesus I break your power of alcohol and drugs over this man's life. I command you to leave him at once and take your addictions with you. Go and trouble him no more.

Immediately, the drunk man became completely sober as if he had never had a drop of alcohol in his life. His face lit up, and he walked away swiftly and steadily, joyously pumping his fists in the air and exclaiming, "Yes! I'm free! I'm free at last!" Praise God! Indeed, he truly was free at last. This was the last time he visited our ministry outreach.

Victory in Christ

God will not overcome sin for us. However, God will give us all the power we need to overcome sin when we use the authority He has given to us to boldly use the name of Jesus in our battle against temptation and sin. Read this again several times.

My friends, we *can* overcome and lead a victorious life in Christ. God would not have asked us to do so if it were not possible. The battle against sin will always be with us, but we can do a *lot* more with God's help to make things *far easier* on ourselves than we are now. Here's a parting scripture for consideration:

> Tremble and *do not sin*; when you are on your
>   beds, *search your hearts* and be silent.
> (Psa. 4:4, emphasis added)

Don't Battle Alone

If you have a binding addiction of any kind in your life, find a Christian who is walking in victory in your area of weakness who will agree with you through prayer in the name of Jesus that the power of the addiction will be broken over your life.

Go forth and live victoriously in the mighty name of Jesus. Be blessed today!

63

How to Pray in Bold Faith That God Answers

AS AN IMMEDIATE FOLLOW-UP on our just-concluded, three-part series on overcoming sin and temptation, let's talk today about our standing before God and the level of faith we need to receive God's miraculous response.

Disclaimer: Those who are trapped in a cycle of known sin should re-read and apply the just-concluded series on overcoming before reading today's devotional lesson.

For those believers who are sinful but are overcomers (none of us are perfect), be honest with yourself as you answer the following questions. When you pray, do you experience any of the following? Do you:

- Feel unworthy before God?
- Hope God is listening or hope He answers?
- See yourself as having such a lowly, distant standing before God that asking Him for what you need such as for miraculous healing for yourself or someone else is a big thing in your eyes?

If the answer to any of these questions is yes, then it is likely you may lack the bold faith needed for God to work miracles on your behalf or possibly even to receive a miracle on your behalf. Allow God to fix this problem today through a careful study of His Word:

> For we do not have a high priest who is unable to empathize with our weaknesses, but we have one who has been tempted in every way, just as we are—yet he did not sin. Let us then approach God's throne of grace *with confidence*, so that we may receive mercy and find grace to *help us* in our time of need. (Heb. 4:15-16, emphasis added)

Our *being* and *feeling* unworthy is one thing, but *acting* and *praying* unworthy is another. Yes, we are unworthy because of our sinful human natures, but when we allow Jesus' blood to cover us that is all our Father God sees. Notice in this scripture that our Father God isn't merely *letting* us come before Him with our requests as an inconvenience to Him. Rather, our Father God actually *wants* us—in fact, *expects* us—to seek His help. Not only that, but He wants us to ask Him with *confidence*. Pretty amazing thought, isn't it?

If we aren't coming before God with confidence, then it's not faith. And if we aren't asking in faith, then we are defeated before we even ask. Is it any wonder, then, that we receive no answer from God?

The Bible is clear: We, believers, are seated *with Christ* at the right hand of our Father, far above evil spirits, sin, and sickness (see Eph. 1:20-21; 2:6). As such, God *wants* us—no, *expects* us—to come before Him in *confidence* to present our requests before Him.

The key to bold faith is to learn to ignore how we *feel* and instead only *act* and *pray* based on what the Word of God says:

> [We] receive from him *anything* we ask, *because we keep his commands* and *do what pleases him.*
> (1 John 3:22, emphasis added)

It has nothing to do with our *feelings* but, rather, everything to do with our *faith* that the Word of God is true and that God will keep His promises. I *know* God is listening to me and will answer my requests simply because God *said He would* in His Word ... *not* because I *feel* that way. My feelings about the matter are irrelevant. I choose to let only what God's Word says count when I pray.

The kind of faith that moves the heart of God to perform on-the-spot miracles on our behalf is the bold faith that *knows* God is listening and *knows* God will respond to our prayers ... not *hopes* God is listening and *hopes* God will respond.

While God's response may not always be what we desire or occur when we want, I see this as a separate matter altogether. When I pray for the miraculous, I *know* God is hearing my prayer, and I *know* He will answer. If God does not answer as I expect or when I expect—and frankly, sometimes, He does not—that has no impact whatsoever on my faith during my next prayer.

If you pray for ten people and *none* of them are healed, then, yes ... then there is a problem. If so, fix it by continuing to let God minister to you through a careful study and application of His Word and these daily devotional messages.

But if you pray for ten people and many but not all of them are healed, then, praise God! Leave it completely up to His sovereignty as to why He did not heal those who weren't healed. Maybe, they will be healed slowly, or later on, or even possibly not at all in this life here on earth. Regardless, none of these negative outcomes have any impact whatsoever on my faith for my next prayer for healing.

We must learn to simply do the works that God asked us to do in full faith and confidence and leave the outcomes up to Him.

Go exercise your *bold faith* today. Set a captive of Satan free today in the name of Jesus!

64

Overcoming Trials Through Worship

WHEN WE ARE HAVING A BAD DAY or in those times when we lose our way, sometimes, the best reaction possible is to drop everything and simply praise God for His goodness and mercy and for who He is.

The following scriptures are intended to help us do just this. Choose to enter into worship today as you read these powerful scriptures from throughout the Bible:

> Before the mountains were born or you brought forth the whole world, from everlasting to everlasting *you are God*. (Psa. 90:2, emphasis added)

> By faith we understand that the universe was formed at God's command, so that what is seen was not made out of what is visible. (Heb. 11:3)

> [God the Father to His Son] He also says, "In the beginning, Lord, you laid the foundations of the earth, and the heavens are the work of your hands. They will perish, but you remain; they will all wear out like a garment. You will roll them up like a robe; like a garment they will be

changed. But you remain the same, and your
years will never end." (Heb. 1:10-12)

Your throne, O God, will last for ever and ever;
　　a scepter of justice will be the scepter of your
　　kingdom. (Psa. 45:6)

Remember the former things, those of long ago;
　　I am God, and there is no other; I am God,
　　and there is none like me.
I make known the end from the beginning, from
　　ancient times, what is still to come.
I say, "My purpose will stand, and I will do all
　　that I please." (Isa. 46:9-10)

... know and believe me and understand that I
　　am he.
Before me no god was formed, nor will there be
　　one after me. (Isa. 43:10)

It is I who made the earth and created mankind
　　on it.
My own hands stretched out the heavens; I
　　marshaled their starry hosts ...
For this is what the Lord says—
he who created the heavens, he is God;
he who fashioned and made the earth, he
　　founded it;
he did not create it to be empty, but formed it to
　　be inhabited—
he says: "I am the Lord, and there is no other ...

By myself I have sworn, my mouth has uttered
in all integrity a word that will not be
revoked:
Before me every knee will bow; by me every
tongue will swear." (Isa. 45:12, 18, 23)

The Lord your God is with you. He is a hero
who saves you.
He happily rejoices over you, renews you with
his love, and celebrates over you with shouts
of joy. (Zeph. 3:17, GWT)

You know when I sit and when I rise; you
perceive my thoughts from afar.
You discern my going out and my lying down;
you are familiar with all my ways.
Before a word is on my tongue you, Lord, know
it completely …
I praise you because I am fearfully and
wonderfully made; your works are
wonderful, I know that full well …
… all the days ordained for me were written in
your book before one of them came to be.
(Psa. 139:2-4, 14, 16)

God saved us and called us to be holy, not because of what we had done, but because of his
own plan and kindness. *Before* the world began,
God *planned* that Christ Jesus would show us
God's kindness. (2 Tim. 1:9, GWT, emphasis
added)

God the Father *knew you long ago* and *chose you* to live holy lives with the Spirit's help so that you are obedient to Jesus Christ and are sprinkled with his blood. May good will and peace fill your lives! (1 Pet. 1:2, GWT, emphasis added)

See what *great love* the Father has lavished on us, that we should be called children of God! *And that is what we are!* (1 John 3:1a, emphasis added)

In closing, I find it difficult to read these scriptures and not break down in praise, worship, and honor to Him who sits on the throne forever and ever ... the Lamb of God, our Lord and Savior, Jesus Christ. I hope your reaction is the same.

When we praise in this manner, our problems fade away, and all that is left is praise and worship and pure communication with God, just as He intended true worship to be.

Be blessed today in all that you do in the mighty name of Jesus!

65

A Glimpse of Heaven

ON SATURDAY, APRIL 17, 2012, at roughly 10 a.m., God gave me a startling vision of heaven. The vision occurred in the middle of my praise and worship, just after I had completed Bible study. I was fully awake and conscious of my surroundings when the vision occurred.

Earth faded into the background. Suddenly, I was standing with a vast, innumerable throng as far as the eye could see, stretching all the way past the distant horizon. A gloriously beautiful song, far more wondrous than the best orchestra music on earth could ever be, swirled around me. I almost immediately noticed with some amazement that, although the music originated from millions of points as far and wide to the horizon as I could see, the melodious notes of the heavenly song arrived from every direction to my ears in perfect sync, despite the sound travel time delay that I normally would presume would be involved with such great distances.

To my amazement, this "song" was not a single melody such as we sing on earth, but rather countless songs. Each song reflected each heavenly singer's unique life story, experiences, and walk with God. Songs of praise from God's people on earth also arose to heaven and were seamlessly mixed in with the heavenly choir. Each song had *meaning* and *feeling* that were conveyed by it. While I instinctively knew I could focus on and listen to any one individual song if I wanted to, I largely did not do so. The collective song was intensely pleasurable and had a collective meaning of praise and worship to God that no individual song or group of songs, however melodious, could ever possibly match. All of the many different individual songs, including mine—although typically different and sung at different times, intervals, and tempos and with unique meanings— nevertheless, all meshed together into a seamless unity of tempo and harmony, becoming a perfectly harmonious song of perfect praise and worship to God the Father and to the Lamb on the throne. How this could be done and sound so perfectly melodious is next to impossible to describe using the limited, crude communication tool available to me: human speech.

As that vast multitude and I lifted up our combined voices in glorious song in praise and worship to God, my attention was drawn upward to a glowing, folding curtain of untold millions of individual, vivid bright colors not far overhead. The colored patterns were moving and folding overhead in perfect, rhythmic sync to our song. Strange though it may sound, all I can do is try to relate what I saw: the lights overhead were *alive*. The lights were synergistically interacting with the song, but not in the manner one might expect. The lights were not interacting with the *rhythm* of the song as is sometimes done electronically here on earth; rather, they were interacting with the heavenly song's *meaning* and intensity of *feeling*. Likewise, I sensed that the lights were interacting with my worship as well. Sure enough, my eyes were soon drawn to a small section of that glorious display that was reacting to my worship uniquely yet in perfect concert with everyone else as well at the same time.

As the intensity of our worship of Him who sits on the throne forever and ever steadily increased, the brilliant display of colors synergistically interacted with our worship to raise our praise still further to new and evermore intense heights of adoration to our Creator God who lives in light eternal. As this process continued, although I had no idea how this could be, I sensed that this ever-increasing synergistic effect between that melodious song and the interactive lights could and in fact *would* literally go on forever.

Perfectly happy and perfectly content, I was filled with peace, love, joy, and complete worship to God the Father and His Son, the Lamb of God, by His side.

I cannot relate what this experience was truly like any better than to simply tell you this: I did not want to go anywhere else, see anything else, hear anything else, do anything else, or know anything else. I literally was perfectly content to permanently remain part of that melodious worship around the throne forever and ever. I never would have left if I had any choice about the matter.

Yet, at the same time, I was dimly aware that I had a family and a life back on earth. However, all that I love so dearly here on this earth—everything that normally seems so important and precious to me—seemed no worthier of further thought there in heaven than my concern for an ant in Africa that is crawling out of its mound, looking for a crumb of food to eat. Everything else seemed so insignificant. I just wanted to get back to perfect peace and praise and worship again! All that I normally love so dearly here on earth was now of no concern to me in heaven whatsoever. My entire being, all that I am, was entirely and totally consumed in harmonious love and worship to God the Father and His Son, Jesus Christ.

As the melodious song and glorious lights began to fade, through the Holy Spirit I *begged* Jesus (who I did not see) to let me stay and worship Him forever and ever. But Jesus replied through the Spirit that I must return to my home and ministry on earth. Jesus told me to "make heaven real to My followers on earth" who He said are far more concerned with the cares of this world than with the incomparably more important reality of heaven.

The vision ended, and I wept hard with both happiness and sorrow at the same time. I was filled with great happiness at what I had just experienced, but I was also filled with great sorrow that I was no longer there.

My friends, heaven is real, and it is happening right now. That melodious song is going on now around the throne of God where all is light, happiness, contentment, peace, love, and joy. No price I could ever be asked to pay here on this cold, dark earth is too much to bear if only I could just be there around the throne once more and hear that melodious song again for even a single minute, never mind being privileged to participate in such unspeakable joy for all eternity. Nothing else matters! Everything else in our world is incomparably insignificant.

Heaven is truly worth the small "price" that Jesus asks us to pay. All Jesus asks of us is to believe in Him as our Lord and Savior and our only Way to God the Father and to allow God to transform us into His Son's image as we renew our minds through the Word of God and His Holy Spirit. These scriptures say it best:

> Since, then, you have been raised with Christ, set
> your hearts on things above, where Christ is,
> seated at the right hand of God. Set your minds
> on things above, not on earthly things.
> (Col. 3:1-2)

Two months later, God showed me another vision of heaven. This time, it was a vision of the heavenly city, the New Jerusalem, followed soon after that by a vision of the end of this world. The latter is a vision which I will relate later in this book.

Are you surprised that God would give His servants such visions? Don't be. Read the Word of God for yourself:

> [The last days] And afterward, I will pour out my
> Spirit on *all people*. Your sons and daughters will
> prophesy, your old men will *dream dreams*, your
> young men will *see visions*. Even on my servants,
> *both men and women*, I will pour out my Spirit *in
> those days*. (Joel 2:28-29, emphasis added)

As I wrote previously in this book, God is no respecter of persons. What God has done for me, He will do for you if you will seek Him with all your heart, soul and mind (Luke 10:25-28).

In conclusion, heaven and hell are real, and both are happening right now. I pray that this experience has helped make heaven more real to you today. Be blessed in the name of Jesus!

(For additional information about this experience and others like it, see the devotionals, "Fire of the Living God Manifested in Us"

and "Glimpse of the End of the World" using the table of contents.)

66

Bold Faith to Rebuke Sin and Wickedness

MOST OF US REMEMBER THE STORY of God's prophet Elijah who defeated 400 prophets of the false god Baal in order to end a severe drought and resulting famine that was upon the land.

However, did you know that the Bible indicates this drought and famine happened because Elijah asked God for it … not because God commanded it? Let's take a look at two scriptures which tell the story:

> Now Elijah the Tishbite, from Tishbe in Gilead, said to Ahab, "As the Lord, the God of Israel, lives, whom I serve, there will be neither dew nor rain in the next few years *except at my word.*"
> (1 Kings 17:1, emphasis added)

Now the story from the New Testament:

> Elijah was a human being, even as we are. *He prayed earnestly* that it would not rain, and it did not rain on the land for three and a half years. *Again he prayed*, and the heavens gave rain, and

the earth produced its crops. (Jam. 5:17-18, emphasis added)

This is another example of God dramatically honoring the bold faith of His servants. As a result of Elijah's faith, the entire nation was led back to God. And there are plenty of other examples in the Bible.

One of the most interesting examples in the Bible of God's servants taking the initiative to rebuke sin and wickedness appears in the *Book of Acts*. Notice how the Apostle Paul took action when Elymas the sorcerer tried to interfere with Paul's efforts to witness to a local government official, the proconsul, Sergius Paulus:

> Elymas the sorcerer ... opposed [Paul] and tried to turn the proconsul from the faith. Then Saul, who was also called Paul, filled with the Holy Spirit, looked straight at Elymas and said ... "Now the hand of the Lord is against you. *You are going to be blind for a time,* not even able to see the light of the sun."
>
> Immediately mist and darkness came over him, and he groped about, seeking someone to lead him by the hand. When the proconsul saw what had happened, *he believed,* for he was amazed at the teaching about the Lord.
> (Acts 13:7-9, 11-12, emphasis added)

This may seem pretty radical by today's standards. However, it illustrates the point again that Jesus has promised to do whatever we ask our Father God to do in His name.

While I have not thought about striking anyone with blindness, I do use the authority in Christ that God has given us to remove obstacles from the path of my witness for Him.

For example, I was in a fairly small swimming pool with a man who I could see was hungry for God, but the nature of our conversation demanded complete privacy. So, I prayed in my mind, "Father God, in the name of your Son, Jesus, don't let anyone come near us until I am finished witnessing to this man." As a result, neither my children nor his or anyone else approached our end of that pool for one hour and 45 minutes. We had it all to ourselves during that time. However, the very minute we finished and began to talk about something else, his children came over.

My fellow believers, what we pray for in faith is what we will receive from God. His Word is faithful and true:

> [Jesus said,] "If you remain in me and my words remain in you, ask *whatever* you wish, and *it will be done for you.*" (John 15:7, emphasis added)

I believe this with all of my heart, and I pray you do, too.

Use your bold faith and set a captive of Satan free today in the name of Jesus! Be blessed.

67

How We Can Know God Will Answer Our Requests

TODAY'S MESSAGE IS A NATURAL extension of yesterday's ending: How can we *know* for certain that God is hearing our prayers and will grant our requests? Such certainty is the result of godly faith, the kind of faith that moves mountains.

So, let's get started. To obtain and retain such absolute confidence (faith) on a regular basis, I recommend closely studying the final parting instructions of our Lord and Savior, Jesus, contained in John 14–17.

This is important because Jesus lived on earth as a man and was tempted not to have faith and to doubt God's promises just like we are tempted. How do we know this? Because the Bible says so:

> For we do not have a high priest who is unable to empathize with our weaknesses, but we have one who has been *tempted in every way, just as we are*—yet he did not sin. (Heb. 4:15, emphasis added)

To build up our faith, then, here are some extremely important final instructions from Jesus found in John, chapter fifteen. Read carefully and prayerfully:

> I am the true vine, and my Father is the gardener. He cuts off every branch in me *that bears no fruit*, while every branch that does bear fruit he prunes so that it will be *even more fruitful* …
>
> I am the vine; you are the branches. *If* you remain in me and I in you, *you will bear much fruit*; apart from me you can do nothing …
>
> *If* you remain in me and my words remain in you, *ask whatever you wish,* and it will be done for you. This is to my Father's glory, *that you bear much fruit*, showing yourselves to be my disciples … *If you keep my* commands, you will remain in my love, just as I have kept my Father's commands and remain in his love … *My command is this*: Love each other as I have loved you … You are my friends **if** you do what I command … This is my command: Love each other.
>
> (John 15:1-2, 5, 7-8, 10, 12, 14, 17, emphasis added)

What does this mean from the context of our faith? Below are several key points extracted from the critical verses above.

We are here to bear fruit—that is, to spiritually reproduce ourselves. If we aren't bearing fruit, we will be cut off. And if we *are* bearing fruit, God wants us to bear more fruit (verse 2).

If we remain in Jesus, we will bear much fruit (verse 5) and keep His commands (verse 10) to love one another as Jesus loves us (verses 12, 14, & 17).

If we do both, we can ask for whatever we want, and it will be done for us (verse 7) for the purpose of our Father's glory—that is, bearing more fruit (verse 8).

So far, so good. Now, let's put it all together in light of the previous devotional reading:

- I was in a swimming pool, witnessing to a man for the purpose of attempting to bear fruit (verse 2);
- Attempting to save someone from hell fire (or physical oppression of his/her body) both qualify as obeying Jesus' command to love one another as He loves us (verses 12, 14, 17);
- My request to God to keep anyone away from our end of the swimming pool because of the particularly private and personal nature of our conversation aligns with the purpose of our Father's glory: bearing more fruit (verse 8);
- Therefore, I knew with absolute certainty, based on the living Word of God, that my Father God had heard my request and had granted it.

Notice that I used the expression *"had* heard and *had* granted it"… not *"will* do it"… because Jesus has left us with instructions on how faith prays:

[Jesus said,] "Therefore I tell you, *whatever* you ask for in prayer, believe that *you have received it,* and it will be yours. (Mark 11:24, emphasis added)

As soon as I asked God, my internal reaction was to know that *it is done in the name of Jesus ... Thank you, Father God! It is finished. End of story. Next subject.*

Jesus tells us that we should pray with absolute certainty based on the living Word of God. This godly conviction (not hope) which is based in scripture (not our own feelings) that Jesus promises will move mountains. Therefore, it should come as no surprise that our Father God delights in answering such prayers

Go use your faith to set a captive of Satan free today in the mighty name of Jesus! Be blessed.

68

Putting Our Faith into Action

WHAT HAPPENS IF WE READ, study, and know what God's Word says about healing the sick, but then we do not do our very best to actually do it? Good question. Let's answer by first listing the deeds that Jesus said believers in Him will *do*:

> Very truly I tell you, whoever believes in me will do the works I have been doing, and they will do even greater things than these, because I am going to the Father. And I will do whatever you ask in my name, so that the Father may be glorified in the Son. You may ask me for anything in my name, and I will do it. (John 14:12-15)

> And these signs will accompany *those who believe*: In my name they will drive out demons; they will speak in new tongues; they will pick up snakes with their hands; and when they drink deadly poison, it will not hurt them at all; they will *place their hands on sick people, and they will get well.* (Mark 16:17-18, emphasis added)

As for the question of what happens if we know what to do but then don't actually *do* it…

> You see that [Abraham's] faith and his actions were working together, and his faith was made complete by what he *did* … You see that a person is considered righteous by what they *do* and not by faith alone. As the body without the spirit is dead, so faith without *deeds* is dead. (Jam. 2:22, 24, 26, emphasis added)

There it is … Faith without action is dead. Useless. Taking a step of faith to actually *do* what Jesus asked us to do isn't always easy, even for those who have done it a lot. It still takes faith and willful effort on our part … often. But *do* it we simply must:

> [Jesus said,] "Very truly I tell you, whoever believes in me will *do* the works I have been doing, and they will *do* even greater things than these, because I am going to the Father. And I will *do* whatever you ask in my name, so that the Father may be glorified in the Son." (John 14:12-13, emphasis added)

Jesus has already promised us up front that He will do whatever we ask in His name for the glory of the Father. But in order for this to happen, we must *do* two things first:

1. We must ask.
2. We must pray expectantly in faith that our requests have been answered.

(Note: Review again the devotional in this book titled, *How We Can Know God Will Answer Our Requests* to learn how we can *know* with absolute *certainty* that God will answer our prayers.)

If we will not ask God or if we ask God but not *expectantly* in faith, God cannot respond with the miraculous. And if we are not doing the works that Jesus called us to do, our faith is dead (Jam. 2:26). And we know that "without faith it is *impossible* to please God" (Heb. 11:6, emphasis added).

So, it all comes down to this: We must not only *hear* the Word of God, but we must *do* what God through His Word has asked us to do. If we listen, study, and read but don't *act*, our combined listening, studying, and reading will count for nothing other than willful self-deception as stated here:

> Do not merely *listen* to the word, and so deceive yourselves. *Do what it says.* (Jam. 1:22, emphasis added)

Here's another one:

> [Jesus said,] "Why do you call me, 'Lord, Lord,' and *do not do what I say*? As for everyone who comes to me and hears my words and puts them into practice, I will show you what they are like. They are like a man building a house, who dug down deep and laid the foundation on rock. When a flood came, the torrent struck that house but could not shake it, because it was well built." (Luke 6:46-48, emphasis added)

I pray that we will not only be listeners and readers of God's Word but that we will not delay in putting into action today what we have been reading for weeks or longer. May God open our eyes to the lost, weary, sick, and dying who are all around us.

Go set a captive of Satan free today in the name of Jesus! Be blessed.

69

How to Pray for
Miraculous Healing (Part 1)

BY WAY OF DEFINITION, I use the terms *miracle* and *miraculous* to distinguish between the natural or medically-assisted healing processes and the instantaneous, on-the-spot, supernatural healings that only God can perform. While any type of healing is greatly preferable to no healing at all, miraculous on-the-spot manifestations of God's power often result in greater glory for the Creator and a greater increase in our faith.

As a follow up to our previous lesson about being doers of the Word of God and not hearers only, today we will begin a three-part series about how we can be used by God to miraculously heal the sick.

When I encounter a sick person I do not know, I ask him or her if I can pray for his or her healing (we will cover family members and friends later on in this series). Most people readily agree because they generally think I intend to pray for them later on somewhere else ... but certainly not in public, right there on the spot.

If the person's answer is "Yes," I immediately pray in the name of Jesus for their healing. Many dramatic, on-the-spot healings happen this way.

If their answer is a confused look or "no," I quote scriptures until the person either declines prayer, physically leaves, or agrees that Jesus *can* heal him or her on the spot.

If the person's answer is an unsure or hesitant "yes," I then give my own personal testimony along with still more scriptures in order to help change their hesitant, "I-think-Jesus-can-heal-me-now" hope (mere wish) into a strong, faith-filled "yes-Jesus-*will*-heal-me-now!" faith confession born of a Holy Spirit inspired *reality.*

What's the difference? Everything.

Notice how Jesus first worked to grow the faith of the father of a demon-possessed son before He then performed the requested miracle:

> [Boy's father] "[The demon] has often thrown [the son] into fire or water to kill him. *But if you can do anything*, take pity on us and help us." "*If you can*?" said Jesus. "*Everything* is possible for one who believes." Immediately the boy's father exclaimed, "I *do believe*; help me overcome my unbelief!" (Mark 9:22-24, emphasis added)

We should do likewise. When we pray prematurely for healing for those who speak unbelief with their lips even innocently, God cannot move on their behalf, and no miracle occurs. Then, the person's faith drops even more, making it harder the next time around ... assuming there ever is a next time. To avoid this, pay close attention to the words that are used by the sick when they request—or, agree to—your intercession for their healing.

Once the sick person's faith confession is right, I then lay hands on the person and tell the sickness, by name, to

leave the person's body in the name of Jesus. I then pronounce the person healed and have him or her give glory to
God. I also have him or her immediately act on their healing
(more on this later in this series).

Because God keeps His promises in His Word, it is no
wonder that God immediately performs the requested miracle according to the faith that has been expressed.

In the next devotional, we will walk step-by-step
through the Biblical scriptures about healing, using actual
healing case examples. A solid understanding of these scriptures is essential in order to have the type of godly faith that
moves mountains.

Be blessed today in the name of Jesus!

70

How to Pray for
Miraculous Healing (Part 2)

LET'S IMAGINE THAT SOMEONE YOU just encountered has just requested prayer for healing, either because you solicited their request or because it was their idea. Your discussion with that individual then proceeds as follows.

> **Believer**: "Jesus said in John 15:16, 'Whatever you ask in my name the Father will give to you.' Do you believe Jesus can heal you right here and right now?"

> **Sick person**: *(hesitantly)* "Y-e-s, but … is it possible in these days?" *(or, "possible for me" or whatever objection is raised)*

> **Believer**: "According to Matthew 8:16-17 and 1 Peter 2:24, Jesus already paid the penalty on the cross 2,000 years ago for our sins, diseases, and infirmities. This is why Jesus said in John 14:12, 'Believers will do the works I do, in fact greater works, because I go to the Father.' That's you and me. You are only claiming Christ's finished work on the cross, which has already been completed

for you. Do you believe Jesus can heal you right here and now?"[1]

Sick Person: "I believe Jesus can do all things." (*This response is generally still short of the level of faith needed, so don't stop here.*)

Believer: "Jesus said in Matthew 9:29, 'Such as *your* faith is so be it done for *you*. Based on my own personal experience of being healed, I know that the Word of God is true. Jesus will heal you now if that is what you want Him to do for you. What is your request? What do you want Jesus to do for you? What do you believe Jesus will do for you personally?"

Sick Person: "I believe Jesus can heal me now. That is what I want from Him. I believe Jesus *will* heal me now."

Believer: "When I lay my hands on you, the power of God will heal you, and you are going to get up and walk."

Sick Person: "I believe this. Yes."

Believer: (*lays hands on the sick person*) "In the name of Jesus, I rebuke (*sickness or infirmity by name*). Leave this body at once and stay gone! Thank you, Father God. You are healed in the name of Jesus. Rise and walk."

In response, the sick person rises and walks, healed on the spot. However, sometimes the sick person reports, "But I don't feel any better."

Believer: "According to the Word of God, you are healed. It is done. You must believe this because the scriptures say it is so, and God's Word is true and does not lie. However, like the healing of the crippled man in Acts 3, and as Jesus said in Mark 11:24, you must believe you are healed first, and the miracle will occur second. You are healed. Since you are healed, now get up and walk." *(believer extends a helping hand)*

Sick Person: *(hesitates ... wanting to believe but unwilling to take action)*

Believer: "In the name of Jesus, you are healed. Don't test your back (or whatever sick/injured body part). I want you to use it to do whatever it is that you couldn't before. Open your lips, give glory to God for your healing, and rise up and walk now in the name of Jesus." *(spoken with authority. Believer begins physically pulling the sick or injured person up as necessary)*

Sick person: *(believes, praises God, rises, and is completely healed)* "Glory to God! I am healed!"

Believer: "Your Father God loves you and has honored your faith. Now, serve Him with new devotion and love. Go and tell everyone what

God has done for you. Study the Bible closely,
and soon, God will use you to heal others."

The preceding dialog is based on many actual healing
cases and is only given as an example to help build your
knowledge of the scriptures and your faith and trust that the
Word of God is true.

While this is one scenario that you will encounter often,
there are other situations where additional scriptures, godly
wisdom, prayer and Holy Spirit perception are required. Finally, you may also encounter situations in which the Holy
Spirit chooses to miraculously heal someone on the spot despite the receiver's doubt or lack of spiritual understanding.
See the final devotional lesson of this book for more information about this type of healing.

In the next devotional we will conclude this series with
a discussion of several less frequently encountered healing
scenarios, including our ministry to family and friends.

Go set a captive of Satan free today in the name of Jesus!
Be blessed.

---

[1] When I pray for unbelievers or adherents of other religions, I keep it
simple. I merely tell them that I believe Jesus is the Son of God and
that I believe my Lord and Savior will heal them if they will agree to
let me pray for them. Most are healed instantly on the spot after
such prayer. Then after they are healed, they typically want to know
all about Jesus. What an opportunity to bring salvation to such people!

71

How to Pray for
Miraculous Healing (Part 3)

WE ARE FREQUENTLY CALLED TO MINISTER to people who are close to us. While you may or may not share my apprehension in this regard, I can find it awkward and challenging, at times, to pray for the healing of close family members, friends, and co-workers who know me well. Part of the problem is because those who know us best also know our faults, struggles, and shortcomings, and of course I am aware that they know. Not only this, but these same individuals likewise realize that I know their faults.

This mutual awareness of each other's shortcomings can combine, at times, to interfere with the bold exercise of our faith.

The solution is straightforward, though it is still easier said than done. When praying for someone close to me, I try to block out everything I know about that individual and ask the Holy Spirit to help me see this person as God our Father sees him; that is, pure and perfect in His sight (if a Christian believer) or a precious human being He has immense love and compassion for (if unsaved). All we can do is address our end of the process.

However, an awareness of our faults is only part of the problem. Let's take a look at the Word of God to try to understand what other variables may be at work. Take a look:

> Coming to his hometown, [Jesus] began teaching the people in their synagogue, and they were amazed. "Where did this man get this wisdom and these miraculous powers?" they asked. "Isn't this the carpenter's son? Isn't his mother's name Mary, and aren't his brothers James, Joseph, Simon and Judas? Aren't all his sisters with us? Where then did this man get all these things?" And they took offense at him.
>
> But Jesus said to them, "A prophet is not without honor except in his own town and in his own home."
>
> And he did not do many miracles there because of their lack of faith. (Matt. 13:54-58)

Even Jesus—the spotless, pure, and perfect Lamb of God—found it difficult to inspire faith from His friends and neighbors in His hometown of Nazareth. Clearly it had nothing to do with faults or imperfections in Jesus, for Jesus never sinned (Hebrews 4:15). Rather, the problem was their shared familiarity with Jesus and knowledge of His upbringing which contributed to their unwillingness to believe.

In like manner, this same dynamic can be at work in our own inner circles. The power of God transforms us daily into entirely new Spirit-filled creations, but those closest to us may continue to see us as they always have. Fortunately, if we consistently live our lives before God in a way that brings honor and glory to Him, those opinions may slowly change.

> [Jesus said,] "Let your light so shine before men, that they may see your good works, and glorify your Father which is in heaven."
> (Matt. 5:16, KJV)

Physical Affliction by Evil Spirits

Another special situation you will encounter from time to time is someone who is physically afflicted not by disease, but rather by the power of Satan. The physical symptoms appear the same, but the cause is not. Wisdom imparted by the Holy Spirit will tell you the difference. When this occurs, instead of rebuking the disease, rebuke the evil spirit that is causing the disease and the individual will be healed.

When No Immediate Healing Occurs

Last but by no means least, another special situation you will likely have to deal with is what to do when someone is not healed immediately. This occurs from time to time for reasons I do not always understand. Perhaps, the person lacks enough faith or will be healed later on, or gradually, or maybe even never. I have no choice but to simply leave the final outcome up to God alone. But I do not let it have any impact whatsoever on my faith when praying for the next individual. With great sensitivity, compassion and understanding to the person who was not healed, I allow God to use me to heal the next person in line.

Finally, a word to those who are so worried about the few who may not get healed that they refuse to be used of

God to heal the many who would be healed if you prayed for them ... does this approach really make sense? I urge you to simply do what our Lord and Savior asked us to do and leave the rest up to Him.

If you pray for ten people and two of them are not immediately healed, simply leave that outcome up to Him. However, if you pray for ten people and *none* of them are healed, then the problem is almost certainly with the person doing the praying.

If this is the case, I suggest resolving the problem by starting this book over from the beginning and re-reading (and applying) everything. Spend the next year immersed in the Bible, memorizing scripture, learning to hear from the Holy Spirit, practicing using your spiritual gifts, and if at all possible being discipled one-on-one by a person who actually *is* being used by God to heal people.

Also, be sure to see final lesson in this book, "Healing Through the Holy Spirit."

Conclusion

In closing, I exhort you not to wait until everything is perfect before you begin ministering to the lost, weary, sick, and injured all around you. If you do, you will never start because Satan will see to it that conditions will never be perfect. I pray that God will open our eyes now to the ripe-for-the-harvest mission field all around us as well as to His heart for souls.

I pray God's blessing upon you as you obey His Word, move forward, and act. Go set a captive of Satan free today in the mighty name of Jesus!

72

Demonstrating Our Faith to Enable Our Miracle

ON A DISTURBINGLY REGULAR BASIS, I notice Christian believers who manage to short-circuit their own miracle by their failure to demonstrate their faith in God and His promises. Although they may say with their mouths that they believe God has heard and granted their request, their actions betray their lack of faith.

To get to the bottom of the problem, let's start by each of us asking ourselves some pointed questions.

What would I do if Jesus Christ stood before me in person and granted my request of Him? Wouldn't I thank Jesus with zeal, run home, and tell everyone I knew what Jesus has done for me? And for you social media enthusiasts, wouldn't your miracle quickly be posted on Facebook, Instagram, Twitter, and everywhere else?

Why then do some of us not react in exactly the same way when we ask God for healing or for whatever miracle? Could it be that some of us do not truly believe we have received from God whatever it is that we have asked God for? Could it be that, inwardly, some of us are still waiting for God to manifest our miracle first *before* we believe?

If so, it is going to be an awfully L-O-N-G wait because God only responds to our faith, which must come first. If we do not or will not believe and demonstrate our faith with our lips and actions, then inwardly, we do not really believe. And if we do not really believe, we do not really have faith. And if we do not have faith, we will not please God (Heb. 11:6) and so we should not expect to receive an answer from God.

To help change this situation, let's re-examine the scriptures that tell us how we should pray for our miracle. Let's start with the instructions given to us by Jesus Himself:

> [Jesus said,] "Therefore I tell you, whatever you ask for in prayer, believe that you *have* received it, and it will be yours." (Mark 11:24, emphasis added)

Here's another important scripture:

> I write these things to you who believe in the name of the Son of God so that you may know that you *have* eternal life. This is the confidence we *have* in approaching God: that if we ask anything according to his will, he hears us. And if we know that he hears us—whatever we ask—we know that we *have* what we asked of him.
> (1 John 5:13-15, emphasis added)

In both scriptures, notice the use of the key word, *have* … as in, we have received our prayer request *now* in the present tense … not *will* have or *may* have in the future tense. Now if we truly believe that we *have* received our request from God, why don't we act like we have received it? Again, do we really believe, or are we just trying to convince ourselves that we believe? If the latter, how can we expect God to grant our request?

Here is a practical example based on a number of actual cases. Each of us should apply this example to ourselves individually as may be applicable. Suppose I have an extremely painful, destroyed knee joint that needs major surgical repair. Further, suppose I have no medical insurance or money to pay for my badly needed knee surgery.

Now suppose a fellow believer in Christ has just laid hands on me and agreed with me in the name of Jesus that I am healed (see the recently concluded series on miraculous healing).

If I truly believe I am healed now, then what I won't do is sit there, waiting for my new knee joint to appear. Why not? Because I know that, according to the Word of God, I already *have* my new knee joint whether I can currently feel or see it or not[1]. Therefore, I make a decision to believe what the Word of God says about my knee rather than what my senses are telling me.

Because I decide to *believe* in faith that I have just received a brand-new knee joint from my Father God, I immediately rejoice, praise God, jump up to my feet, and take off running to show everyone my healed new knee.

When I jump up and *use* my brand new knee joint—notice the emphasis on the word *use*... not *test*—because I *know* my new knee is there simply and only because the Word of God says it is there, and *not* because I am waiting to feel or see it first—now *this* is the kind of godly faith that moves mountains.

And, guess what? In that instant, my brand-new knee joint indeed *is* there, and I physically *am* healed, just as I already knew beforehand from scripture was the case. God is pleased when we choose to believe what His Word says instead of our human senses or any other distractions that may happen.

Just as Jesus said, our miracle will follow our belief. Our miracle will occur in the spiritual realm first and the physical realm second.

Likewise, the same is true with every other type of miracle for which we ask from God.

To help strengthen and confirm our faith still further in the next devotional reading, we will review two miraculous answers to prayer: a physical healing and a financial miracle.

Be blessed and encouraged today in the name of Jesus!

---

[1]On many occasions God chooses to heal His children instantly, just as soon as the request is made. But on other occasions God waits to see if we believe what we are asking for. This lesson applies to this latter case.

73

Personal Testimonies Demonstrating Faith for the Miraculous

SHARING OUR PERSONAL TESTIMONIES with each other helps to build up and confirm our mutual faith. In this devotional reading, I will share two miraculous answers to prayer: a physical healing and a financial miracle.

Physical Healing

Over a two-week period in February 2012, I asked God repeatedly to restore my eye vision so I could see clearly without having to wear eyeglasses.

Nine years before right when I turned forty, my vision had fallen off a cliff. Ever since then I had needed to wear prescription glasses in order to read and drive, particularly in low light. Now at forty-nine, my motive behind my request for healing was not to test God or because I didn't want to wear glasses anymore. Rather, it was because I had a blind colleague who worked for me and I wanted God to grow my faith so I could believe for my blind colleague's healing by first receiving healing for my own poor vision.

However, despite my multiple earnest prayers, my vision remained unchanged. There was no apparent response from God to my prayers of faith.

Finally, I asked God one night why He had not healed my eyesight in accordance with His promises in His Word. Immediately, the Holy Spirit flashed a picture in my mind of my prescription eyeglasses that were in my jacket pocket at that moment.

I understood the Holy Spirit's message: I had been hanging on to my prescription eyeglasses because, somewhere deep inside me, keeping my prescription glasses around was my backup plan in case God didn't heal my vision.

It was time to demonstrate my faith. Did I believe God was going to heal my vision or not?

On the spot, I took out my prescription eyeglasses, dropped them to the sidewalk, broke up the lenses and frames, and threw away the pieces. I then prayed, "Father God, I receive my healed vision in the name of your Son, Jesus. Thank you, Father!" Just like that, my reading vision was restored and became sharp and clear. I have been reading and driving without eyeglasses ever since for more than eight years since through the publication date of this book. Thank you, God! This tremendous blessing significantly increased my faith to believe for and pray for even bigger miracles. However, my blind employee declined my offer to pray for his healing[1].

Each time we are confronted with an opportunity to use our faith, God is putting us in a position where we can either increase our faith or allow it to decline. Don't wait, my friends! Use the faith you already have now in order to grow your faith (this is the principle that is expressed in Matthew 25:14-30).

Financial Miracle

Starting a new consulting business or any type of business is seldom an easy matter that goes exactly as planned. In early July of 2011, due to a business failure my wife Michelle and I found ourselves urgently needing a financial miracle. We were left with two choices: doubt God or trust God. We chose to believe in the instructions given to us by Jesus when He was on earth (see the previous devotional reading):

> [Jesus said,] "Therefore I tell you, whatever you ask for in prayer, *believe that you have received it,* and it will be yours." (Mark 11:24, emphasis added)

We chose to follow the instructions of Jesus exactly as written. Knowing that our words are powerful and that we must both "believe in our hearts" and "speak with our lips" (Rom. 10:9) in order to express our faith, I went to see our apartment complex assistant manager where we lived at that time. Trusting in God with all of my heart, I boldly used my lips to tell the assistant property manager that my God would provide what we needed to pay our rent before her 72-hour eviction notice could take effect. I ended by reciting this scripture to our assistant property manager:

> And my God will meet all your needs according to the riches of his glory in Christ Jesus. (Phil. 4:19)

At that very moment, I looked past the assistant property manager through her office window and noticed that the postal mail carrier had arrived at our community mailboxes. Stirred in my spirit, I left her office to check the mail, only to discover a completely unexpected check for $5,000 that had been sent by someone in another state who wrote that he thought we might be able to use the funds!

Thanking God, I turned around and went right back into the assistant manager's office again, holding up the $5,000 check as I came in. She was amazed and gave glory to God. This gave me an opportunity to share my personal testimony with her, which helped her to increase her own faith in God and in His Word.

Conclusion

Fellow believers, some of you at this late point in this book still continue to be amazed or even doubt that God will perform miracles like this for His children, and above all you doubt that He will do so for you. Please think again. After all, Jesus did tell us what our Father God will do if we ask in His Son's name:

> [Jesus said,] "You did not choose me, but I chose you and appointed you so that you might go and bear fruit—fruit that will last—and so that *whatever you ask in my name the Father will give you*." (John 15:16, emphasis added)

"Whatever I ask." I believe in Jesus' promise exactly as written here with all of my heart, soul, and mind ... not because I bother to try to "understand" what can't be understood, but simply because my Lord and Savior said it. And to no surprise at all, true to His Word, our Father God indeed does honor the exercise of our simple faith. (For more on the subject of simple faith, see the devotional reading on this topic in this book titled, "Simple Faith Like a Child's that Can Move Mountains.")

What God has done for me, He is eager to do for you. Believe the promises of our loving Father God and *act* on them. Go set a captive of Satan free today in the mighty name of Jesus! Be blessed.

---

[1]Interestingly enough, he stated that his life was rich and full as it was already, and so he was content to remain without vision.

74

Why God Requires
Us to Have Faith

DO YOU EVER WONDER WHY God places so much importance on our faith? In fact, do you ever wonder why God requires us to have faith in Him in the first place? Going even further, do you ever wish God would visibly show Himself to us so we will not need so much faith ... or even, any faith ... in order to believe?

Why can't things be like they were in the Old Testament days of the Bible when God visibly appeared to His people with many dramatic manifestations of His divine glory, including fire from heaven and His visible presence appearing in the Most Holy place of the tabernacle.

Let's examine what has changed between the Old and New Testaments of the Bible and how this applies to us and our faith today.

Old Testament

In the Old Testament age, God counted His people as righteous if they obeyed His Law, as stated in these scripture passes:

Moses writes this about the righteousness that is by the law: "And if we are careful to obey all this law before the Lord our God, as he has commanded us, that will be our righteousness." (Deu. 6:25)

Clearly no one who relies on the law is justified before God, because "the righteous will live by faith." The law is not based on faith; on the contrary, it says, "The person who does these things will live by them." (Gal. 3:11-12)

In other words, God's people obtained God's favor and blessings simply by keeping the Law, with little mention made about the actual condition of their hearts. That was the easy part for them.

Of course, back in those days, Christ hadn't yet come as an offering for sin, either. So, God's people had to offer animal sacrifices on an ongoing basis in order to atone for their sins. This was the hard part for them.

To sum things up, in that age obtaining God's favor was automatic (the easy part) as long as God's people took care to obey the Law fully (the hard part for them).

Our situation is reversed today. Let's see how.

New Testament

In this New Testament age, God counts the thoughts of our minds on our inside as well as our actions on the outside.

[In reference to Exodus 20:14, Jesus said,], "You have heard that it was said, 'You shall not commit adultery.' But I tell you that anyone who

looks at a woman lustfully has already committed adultery with her in his heart."
(Matt. 5:27-28)

Because of this and other requirements like it given by
Jesus in the New Testament, God's standards of righteous-
ness for us today are incredibly higher than before in the
Old Testament. This is the hard part for us.

However, praise God the Father for His wondrous plan
of salvation for us! His Son, Jesus, is our one-time sacrifice
for our sins in the past, present, and future as stated here:

[Referring to Jesus] But when this priest had offered for all time one sacrifice for sins, he sat
down at the right hand of God ... For by *one sacrifice* he has *made perfect forever* those who are being made holy. (Heb. 10:12, 14, emphasis added)

Referring to salvation through obeying the Law (termed
"works"), the Apostle Paul explained what we must do instead of works in order for us to be saved today:

... to the one who does not work but trusts God
who justifies the ungodly, *their faith is credited as
righteousness.* (Rom. 4:5, emphasis added)

No faith equals no salvation. Once again, we see the critical importance of our faith in our salvation and in our daily
walk with God.

Today, obtaining God's favor requires faith (the hard
part for us) in God and Jesus Christ's one-time sacrifice for
our sins in which He did all of the work (the easy part for

us), eliminating our need for animal sacrifices. This is the reverse of life under the old covenant in the Old Testament.

Conclusion

Obviously, it would not require much faith for us to believe if we could see God's visible glory shining out of the Most Holy Place of the tabernacle every time we looked that way. Because this is not the case today, then everything rests upon our faith.

Faith in what we cannot see is the hard part for us today. Unfortunately, it seems some believers would almost rather go back to offering animal sacrifices than learn to have faith in God and His promises.

I earnestly pray that your faith and trust in God will not come with difficulty. Instead, I pray that your faith in God and in the promises in His Word will grow stronger and stronger with every passing day as you exercise the faith you have now. Be blessed today in the name of Jesus!

75

Zeal for God and His Kingdom

AS CHRISTIANS, WE ARE OFTEN fired up about sports, shopping, friends, family, our careers, and other earthly things we deem important. But do we have an even greater zeal for our living God? If not, why not? What can we do to regain or keep God in His proper place as the object of our greatest love and strongest desire?

Zeal for God and His Kingdom can be simply summed up as loving the things that God loves and hating the things that God hates. Let's see what the Word of God says about our zeal for God.

> Never be lacking in zeal, but keep your spiritual fervor, serving the Lord. (Rom. 12:11)

> … for zeal for your house consumes me, and the insults of those who insult you fall on me. (Psa. 69:9)

> Do I not hate those who hate you, Lord, and abhor those who are in rebellion against you?
> I have nothing but hatred for them; I count them my enemies. (Psa. 139:21-22)

Notice from the book of Revelation how God weighs us in the balance and wants us to retain our first love of Him:

> [Jesus to the church at Ephesus] I know your deeds, your hard work and your perseverance. I know that you cannot tolerate wicked people, that you have tested those who claim to be apostles but are not, and have found them false. You have persevered and have endured hardships for my name, and have not grown weary.
>
> Yet I hold this against you: You have *forsaken the love you had at first*. Consider how far you have fallen! Repent and *do the things you did at first*. If you do not repent, I will come to you and remove your lampstand from its place. (Rev. 2:2-5, emphasis added)

The creeping contamination of the world around us can, without our notice, stealthily erode our spiritual zeal for God. Once our zeal for God has slipped or is gone, we are left with wondering if and how we can get it back.

Fortunately, Jesus told us exactly how we can regain our zeal for God:

> But seek first his kingdom and his righteousness, and all these things will be given to you as well. (Matt. 6:33)

Each and every day, we are faced with the same choice all over again: Will we put God first in our day, or will we let other distractions in our lives distract us?

How we start our day has a great deal to do with what is first and foremost in our lives: the living God or being busy tending to the things of this world.

For tips and pointers about how we should start our day every day, see the devotional lesson titled, "Putting God First in Our Day."

If you would like to make God your highest pursuit and greatest love in your life, pray this prayer from your heart and mean it:

> Father God, teach me to love the things You love and to hate the things You hate. Forgive me for being distracted by other things. I commit to putting You first and foremost in my day every day from now on. May You be first and foremost above all else in my life from now on. Restore my zeal and passion for You! Thank You, Father God. In the name of your Son, Jesus. Amen.

My friends, this is a prayer that our God will always answer above and beyond our expectations. Satan will test our commitment, but pray this prayer every day if you have to until you form godly habits to start your day. God will bless you for your perseverance. Our *commitment* is only a start; it is our ongoing daily *actions* that count.

Make this commitment from your heart today, mean it and stick with it. Be blessed in the name of Jesus.

76

Breaking the Cycle of Unworthiness and Unanswered Prayer

HAVE YOU EVER FELT SO UNWORTHY before God that it interfered with your worship, prayer life, and faith? Most of us, at some point or another, including myself, have experienced this before in our walk with God. In fact, it is likely that some of you reading this are feeling this way right now.

When this state occurs, we can allow ourselves to feel so unworthy that it can be difficult if not impossible for us to claim God's promises in faith on our behalf. Then, once we are finally forced by circumstances to ask God for His help anyway, our faith under such circumstances is generally weak, faltering, and ineffective. Our lack of faith prevents God from being able to responding to our requests.

Of course, unanswered prayer, in turn, can further increase our sense of unworthiness before the Lord, making the problem even worse. And so, the cycle repeats and intensifies over time. Speaking for myself, I strongly struggled with this condition for many years until a few years ago. In fact, I still occasionally struggle with it now.

In order to help correct this problem, here are some powerful scriptures from God's Word on the subject. I pray the Holy Spirit will open our minds as we read God's thoughts for each of us who reads this:

> God the Father *knew you long ago and chose you* to live holy lives with the Spirit's help so that you are obedient to Jesus Christ and are sprinkled with his blood. May good will and peace fill your lives! (1 Pet. 1:2, GWT, emphasis added)

We serve an amazing Father God who has already foreseen *everything* there is that's bad about us, and yet who still chooses us to serve Him in Christ anyway. Not only this, but we serve a God who has equipped us with His Spirit so that we can serve Him properly and in faith, just as He desires.

Think about it ... We are God's chosen people, both individually and collectively. We can see this again in this scripture:

> But you are a *chosen people*, a royal priesthood, a holy nation, God's special possession, that *you* may declare the praises of him who called *you* out of darkness into his wonderful light.
> (1 Pet. 2:9, emphasis added)

God wants us to believe this and to act accordingly. We know this because God couldn't emphasize any more strongly how He wants us to view ourselves than by what He has told us in the following three scriptures:

> Therefore, there is now *no condemnation* for those who are in Christ Jesus ... Who will bring *any charge* against those whom God has chosen? It is

God who justifies. Who then is the one who condemns? *No one.* Christ Jesus who died—more than that, who was raised to life—is at the right hand of God and is also *interceding for us.*
(Rom. 8:1, 33-34, emphasis added)

For we do not have a high priest who is unable to empathize with our weaknesses, but we have one who has been tempted in every way, just as we are—yet he did not sin. Let us then approach God's throne of grace *with confidence,* so that we may receive mercy and find grace to help us in our time of need. (Heb. 4:15-16, emphasis added)

For by one sacrifice he has *made perfect forever* those who are being made holy. (Heb. 10:14, emphasis added)

Finally, let's be clear that there is a big difference between being sinful but living in the process of overcoming sin versus being sinful but dwelling in sin and not overcoming. Those who want to find a way to justify their sins will always find a way to do so. This message is not aimed at those who are content to live in sin, but rather at those who are overcomers saved by grace. Only God and ourselves know the difference.

While we are, in fact, unworthy to stand before God, the righteous covering blood of Jesus over us makes us pure, holy, and righteous in God's sight. In fact, God views us as if we have never sinned, just the way He views His Son, Jesus Christ. Thank you, Jesus, for Your perfect sacrifice for us!

My friends, come *boldly* before the throne of our Father God today and ask for what you need in full faith, trust, and confidence in the one-time, perfect atoning sacrifice of our Lord and Savior, Jesus Christ.

Be blessed today in the name of Jesus.

77

Revelation Rewards for Being Victorious

TODAY, WE WILL CONFINE OUR Bible study entirely to the often under-appreciated book of Revelation. This message is a natural follow up to the previous discussion about zeal for God.

Today, we live in a time when God's grace, mercy, and forgiveness are discussed far more than the topics of sin, overcoming, God's justice, and the judgments of hell ... if these subjects are ever mentioned at all. Although *hellfire* is discussed more in the Bible than *heaven*, it isn't in style to discuss "unpleasant subjects" in many of today's most popular churches. Accordingly, significant critical portions of the Word of God are intentionally and deliberately not taught in such churches.

Nevertheless, it is abundantly clear from a study of the unabridged Bible that it is our actions—not just our intentions, commitments, and heart alone—that count to God. It also is clear that God has very high expectations of us in terms of our actions and that there are major consequences for us if we do not meet those expectations.

Take a look at Jesus' strong emphasis on our deeds and not just on His forgiveness:

> I know your *deeds*, your love and faith, your service and perseverance, and that you are now *doing* more than you did at first … I am he who searches hearts and minds, and I will repay each of you according to your *deeds*. (Rev. 2:19, 23, emphasis added)

Jesus lists seven reasons in the book of Revelation why our actions count, along with seven rewards that the victorious will receive. In this message, we have space only to cover the latter. However, read in your Bibles for the full context of both.

The seven heavenly rewards for the victorious:

> To the one who is *victorious*, I will give the right to eat from the tree of life, which is in the paradise of God. (Rev. 2:7b, emphasis added)

> The one who is *victorious* will not be hurt at all by the second death. (Rev. 2:11b, emphasis added)

> To the one who is *victorious*, I will give some of the hidden manna. I will also give that person a white stone with a new name written on it, known only to the one who receives it. (Rev. 2:17, emphasis added)

> To the one who is *victorious* and does my will to the end, I will give authority over the nations—that one "will rule them with an iron scepter and will dash them to pieces like pottery"—just as I have received authority from my Father. I will

also give that one the morning star. (Rev. 2:26-28, emphasis added)

The one who is *victorious* will ... be dressed in white. I will never blot out the name of that person from the book of life, but will acknowledge that name before my Father and his angels. (Rev. 3:5, emphasis added)

The one who is *victorious* I will make a pillar in the temple of my God. Never again will they leave it. I will write on them the name of my God and the name of the city of my God, the new Jerusalem, which is coming down out of heaven from my God; and I will also write on them my new name. (Rev. 3:12, emphasis added)

To the one who is *victorious*, I will give the right to sit with me on my throne, just as I was victorious and sat down with my Father on his throne. (Rev. 3:21, emphasis added)

Be victorious!

As we have just seen, victory is the repeated refrain spoken by Jesus Himself to us in Revelation 2 and 3. It would be a fearful day indeed if Jesus ever said about us what He said about the backslidden church of Sardis:

I have found your deeds *unfinished* in the sight of my God. (Rev. 3:2, emphasis added)

Let us finish the race that is in front of us. As we can see from the seven rewards offered to us by Jesus in the book of Revelation, this is a race that is well-worth finishing.

Be victorious today in the name of Jesus! Be blessed.

78

How to Get a Pay Raise or a Better Job

BECAUSE I DO A LOT OF career counseling both as part of my job and also through my church and ministry, I hear these kinds of problems a lot:

- I can't stand my boss! Agree with me in prayer that I will find a better employer.

- I just can't find the right job. My bosses just won't recognize my skills and the value I bring to the table.

- I prayed in faith for a better job, and I thought I had it ... But it turns out that the working environment at my new job is just as bad as it was at my last job.

In reply, I generally ask some variation of this question: "Could it be that you are bringing the problem with you to each new boss and each new employer?"

I ask this question because the Word of God contains an insightful solution to the above problems. However, most of us will not like God's solution at first. Are you ready?

Here is God's plan for us "wage slaves" to get that pay raise, promotion, or new job for which we have been earnestly believing God:

> Slaves, obey your earthly masters with *respect and fear*, and with sincerity of heart, *just as you would obey Christ.* Obey them not only to win their favor when their eye is on you, but as slaves of Christ, doing the will of God *from your heart.* Serve wholeheartedly, *as if you were serving the Lord, not people.* (Eph. 6:5-7, emphasis added)

I know this is not what you wanted to hear. This can be a very rough scripture just to read, never mind accept or apply to our lives. I know firsthand because, many years ago, this scripture burned me badly also.

In the late 1990's, I worked for a fairly well-known software development company as a team leader of that company's rapid development software test engineering group. I was in a spot in my job where I felt insulted and neglected by my superiors because my salary was far lower than it should have been, considering my high-performance reviews as the company's widely acknowledged top test engineer.

So, I went on a year-long campaign to "make the company treat me right" as I thought of it then. Sound familiar? Every day, I came to work and complained to anyone who would listen—and many who wouldn't—about how badly my boss was treating me by not giving me a large salary adjustment. Too valuable to fire, I felt I could say whatever I wanted to embarrass my boss. So, I did just that every chance I got.

Additionally, I also had my church family of that time praying for me. But nothing I did worked for a year.

Finally, I had a particularly ugly, loud ungodly shouting match one day with my boss at work that everyone either heard themselves or soon learned about. As he had before, my boss continued to adamantly refuse to give me a salary adjustment or even a pay raise, without giving me good reasons why not.

Completely discouraged, the next day I turned to the Word of God. Asking God to give me an answer once and for all, I opened my Bible and my eyes fell upon Ephesians 6:5-7 (quoted above).

At first, I rebelled with seething anger against God. But soon, I repented to God of my evil thoughts and horrible conduct toward my boss. I then had the absolutely humiliating task of not only apologizing sincerely and earnestly to my boss but also to everyone in my company who had heard me complain or shout at my boss. That was a lot of apologizing!

Guess what? My boss not only forgave me, but we became friends that day. In fact, we remain respectful and supportive of each other over twenty years later to this day.

A month after I sincerely apologized, my boss beamed with pride as he gave me a huge 20% pay raise plus 3,250 shares of company stock worth about $250,000 at the time. He told me,

> Paul, I've always admired your work, but I didn't respect you personally because you didn't respect me as your boss. Now that you honor me with the Christian spirit you always talk about, I

now respect both you *and* your work, so I am
happy to show you how valuable you are to me.

Ouch! But once again, the Word of God was proven
true, even the most difficult-to-accept parts of it.

I pray that you read these words in the helpful spirit in
which they are intended. Read Ephesians 6:5-7 (quoted
above) with new eyes as you ask God who knows the
thoughts of your heart if you have some repenting to do for
your thoughts and actions toward your current or past em-
ployers. God will bless, reward, and promote you as you are
faithful to obey His Word.

Be blessed today in the name of Jesus!

79

Seeking the Lord with All Our Heart and Soul

LET'S TALK ABOUT SEEKING GOD with everything we have. Let's start by reading scripture:

> If ... you seek the Lord your God, you will find him *if* you seek him with *all of your heart* and with *all of your soul*. (Deut. 4:29, emphasis added)

> ... for the eyes of the Lord range throughout the earth to strengthen those whose hearts are *fully committed* to him. (2 Chron. 16:9a, emphasis added)

Just what does "fully committed" mean? Here is David's touching prayer of full commitment to God:

> One thing I ask from the Lord, this only do I
> seek:
> that I may dwell in the house of the Lord all the
> days of my life,
> to gaze on the beauty of the Lord and to seek
> him in his temple. (Psa. 27:4)

We all know how far away God can seem at times when we are earnestly seeking Him. When this happens, Psalm 77 can help a great deal. First, notice how far away God seems, followed by the breakthrough solution a few verses later:

> I cried out to God for help; I cried out to God to hear me.
> When I was in distress, I sought the Lord; at night I stretched out untiring hands, and I would not be comforted.
> I remembered you, God, and I groaned; I meditated, and my spirit grew faint ...
> Then I thought, "To this I will appeal: the years when the Most High stretched out his right hand.
> I will remember the deeds of the Lord; yes, I will remember your miracles of long ago.
> I will consider all your works and meditate on all your mighty deeds."
> Your ways, God, are holy. What god is as great as our God?
> You are the God who performs miracles; you display your power among the peoples.
> (Psa. 77:1-3, 10-14)

In other words, we should begin our search for God by taking the time to recall and meditate on what He has already done for us. This is not a wasted effort, for God promises us success when we seek Him with everything we have:

> You will seek me and find me *when* you seek me with *all* your heart. (Jer. 29:13, emphasis added)

[Jesus said,] "For *everyone* who asks receives; the one who seeks finds; and to the one who knocks, the door will be opened." (Luke 11:10, emphasis added)

God asks us not to delay. Let us not put off our pursuit of God until another more convenient time that may never come, but rather, let us seek the Lord today:

Seek the Lord while he may be found; call on him while he is near. (Isaiah 55:6)

Today if you hear his voice, do not harden your hearts ... (Hebrews 3:7-8)

The Lord is nearby today. Seek Him with all of your heart today, and you will find Him. Be blessed in the name of Jesus!

80

Fire of the Living God Manifested in Us

HAVE YOU EVER WISHED TO experience the power of God? Have you ever wondered what it would be like to experience a taste of God's glory here on earth? Have you ever wished for the Holy Spirit to take you over completely?

Or, might you have experienced the power of God in the past but haven't in a while, and you long to experience Him again?

If the answer to any of these questions is *yes*, this devotional message is for you. Let's explore how all born-again Christians can seek the manifest presence and glory of God.

Worship brings us into God's presence.

Throughout the Bible, we can see the power of music to aid us in coming into the presence of God. Nowhere is this more vividly described than when King Jehoshaphat of Judah inquired of the Lord through the prophet Elisha:

> Elisha said, "... bring me a harpist." While the harpist was playing, the hand of the Lord came on Elisha and he [prophesied the word of the Lord]. (2 Kings 3:14-16)

Today, uplifting music can be played through an electronic device, performed on a musical instrument or sung with your lips from your heart. Praise and worship music is ideal, but even instrumental music can help to bring us into His presence as it uplifts, exalts and glorifies our amazing all-powerful God and His Son Jesus.

If we pursue God with all of our hearts, we will find Him. The Holy Spirit will always come upon those who seek Him (Luke 11:13); what happens after that depends upon what the Holy Spirit wants to do and our degree of decision to yield fully to Him.

Enter into God's presence.

Here is what I do to seek and experience God's presence in a mighty, tangible way.

First, after Bible study and prayer, I put aside everything in my busy life, then in a quiet place by myself I play the beautiful music and lyrics of an uplifting and sacred worship song play in the background. Here is a thought about worship music that is worth pondering carefully, dear friends: our music must *lead* us into worship of our living God, and not be a *substitute* for our worship. And in regard to our choice of worship music, is your focus on what music does the Holy Spirit like, or is your focus on what music *you* like?

Next, devoting all of my thoughts and attention to God alone, I pray a prayer such as this from my heart and mean it:

Father God, in the name of your Son Jesus, make
your glory and your presence manifest in me as
I enter into heartfelt worship of You.

As I listen and enter into praise and worship of our all-powerful, all-loving God who lives forever and ever, the presence of God draws near. As the Holy Spirit begins to fall on me, I lift my hands in worship, and the Holy Spirit flows through me in heavenly tongues of praise and worship to our God and His Son Jesus.

As I surrender completely in tears of joy, the power of the Holy Spirit begins to overwhelm me physically, starting with my legs and hands and moving up my body until I am physically helpless, unable to move, and prostrate in worship to our mighty God.

Each person's experience with the Holy Spirit will be different, particularly in the beginning and depending on which spiritual gifts of the Holy Spirit has given individually us (1 Corinthians 12). As my worship rises still higher and higher, God's power intensifies upon me. Here is what it often becomes like for me.

The music fades away, and I am caught up out of my senses of this world. The Holy Spirit may rest upon me, communicating intimately with my spirit while my tongue overflows in heavenly praise. From here, the Holy Spirit may visually show me scenes of important events that are happening in a faraway place right at that very moment, or He may show me events in vivid detail that will occur in a few days or in the distant future. Very frequently, the Holy Spirit will draw my attention to specific people for whom God prepares me to minister in advance to. Later on, when

I later encounter these same individuals in the same locations the Holy Spirit showed me they would be, they are dressed in the same clothes that God showed me in advance they would be wearing.

The level of joy, peace, happiness, contentment, trust, and amazing love from our Father God is so perfect and complete that I literally could stay right there worshipping in God's presence forever and ever if it were my choice.

The glory of God can be so overpowering that it can be very difficult to comprehend—never mind accept—the lifting of the Holy Spirit's presence as the return to everyday life occurs. Often, I have shed bitter tears at finding myself, once again, back in this cold, dark world.

Heaven is well worth seeking.

As I wrote in a previous devotional lesson in this book titled "A Glimpse of Heaven," paradise is truly worth everything God asks of us and far, far more. It is simply beyond any human description.

As God says to us in His own words,

> You will seek me and find me *when* you seek me
> with *all* your heart. (Jer. 29:13, emphasis added)

The sooner we start seeking God, the sooner we will find Him. Let us make a lasting commitment now to pursue our God daily with all of our hearts, souls, minds, and bodies.

May you be richly blessed in the Lord, far beyond all of your expectations as you seek Him with a fervent passion today!

Be blessed in the mighty name of Jesus!

81

Mastering Your Crisis (Part 1)

What to Do When Everything Goes Wrong

WE'VE ALL HAD BAD DAYS and tough times. However, I'm sure we can all agree that nothing we have ever experienced or can imagine could be worse than being beaten, tortured, and publicly crucified to death in front of your mother and best friends as the penalty for billons of awful sins you didn't commit ... all at the hands of the very people you created, love passionately, and came to serve, save, and take to heaven if only they would consent. This was the ultimate bad day.

How Jesus handled this ultimate crisis contains deeply insightful lessons for each of us individually as we each go through our own lesser but still tough crises and hard times in life. Jesus is a worthy example for us in everything because, although He was the Son of God, we must remember that our Savior suffered as a human being exactly as we do, according to the scriptures:

> For we do not have a high priest who is unable to empathize with our weaknesses, but we have one who has been tempted in every way, *just as we are*—yet he did not sin. (Heb. 4:15, emphasis added)

So, how did Jesus endure suffering as a human like us? Our biggest clue comes from the words of Jesus Himself:

> [Jesus said,] "A time is coming and in fact has come when you will be scattered, each to your own home. You will leave me all alone. Yet I am not alone, *for my father is with me.* (John 16:32, emphasis added)

Jesus *knew* His Father was with Him and *knew* His Father would never leave Him. He was sure of this even when His humanity didn't feel that way and although He couldn't see His Father. Jesus knew His Father was with Him because of the same way we can know our Father God is with us—that is, because God says so in His Word ... that's why. Jesus had carefully studied the Word of God of His day, the Old Testament, and knew what His Father has promised to us all:

> The Lord himself goes before you and will be with you; *he will never leave you nor forsake you.* Do not be afraid; do not be discouraged. (Deut. 31:8, emphasis added)

If we view our Heavenly Father as being far away in heaven, it will be natural to feel overwhelmed when we are tested by trials and crises. But if we can ever grasp a vision of the reality of the nearness of God to us and within us, that reality will begin to change everything about our trust and faith in God as well as how we pray and speak with our mouths as we go through our crises.

Just how near is our God to us? Read the words of Jesus for yourself:

[Jesus said,] "I will not leave you as orphans; I will come to you. Before long, the world will not see me anymore, but you will see me. Because I live, you also will live. On that day you will *realize* that I am in my Father, and you are in me, and *I am in you*. Whoever has my commands and keeps them is the one who loves me. The one who loves me will be loved by my Father, and I too will love them and *show myself to them*. (John 14:18-21, emphasis added)

Two chapters later, Jesus explained what to do when we are faced with trouble in this life:

[Jesus said,] "I have told you these things, so that in me you may *have peace*. In this world *you will have trouble*. But take heart! I have overcome the world. (John 16:33, emphasis added)

Jesus bluntly warned us that troubles will befall us all. Nevertheless, Jesus was equally clear with us that we are to "have peace" in Him despite it all. As a Pastor of a church my family and I once attended would observe from time to time, "Jesus had the worst day of His life so that you could have the best days of your life." So true! That is ... depending on what our priorities are, of course. If our priorities are the things of this world, the thought that Jesus is literally with us and in us right now may not comfort us that much, if at all.

But for those who are obeying Jesus' command to "seek first his kingdom and his righteousness, and all these things will be given to you as well" (Matt. 6:33), this is truly a very comforting thought indeed ... even in the midst of our worst crises.

Each of us must know by faith that God is literally right here with us, individually, right now. This is the reality of which each of us can ask God to open our minds to right now.

Carefully meditate on this scripture about what happened when Elisha the prophet prayed for his servant who was frightened by enemy soldiers that had surrounded their city to capture and kill them:

> And Elisha prayed, "Open (my servant's) eyes, Lord, so that he may see." Then the Lord opened the servant's eyes, and he looked and saw the hills full of horses and chariots of fire all around Elisha. (2 Kings 6:17)

Are your eyes open? Do you see your troubles all around you? Or do you see God and His angels all around you? What you see by faith is what you will have.

I pray that your eyes have been opened and that God will use this message to encourage your faith and trust in Him today.

For additional important scriptures and information about how to survive the tests and trials of life, see the prior devotionals in this book on this subject entitled "Conquering Obstacles in Our Path" and "Our Authority in Christ (Revisited)."

Be encouraged in the name of Jesus in all you do and say today! You are blessed. If you believe this by faith, then pray, talk, and act like it. God is faithful to honor His Word, so we know by faith that, in due season, we will reap if we are faithful and tend to our Father's business:

> And let us not be weary in well doing: for in due season we shall reap, if we faint not.
> (Gal. 6:7 KJV)

Praise the Lord! Amen.

82

Mastering Your Crisis (Part 2)

Perseverance Through Trials

IT IS NATURAL FOR US to dislike turmoil and crisis and to ask God to spare us from such difficulty. While a fair amount of our troubles here on this earth are caused directly or indirectly by our own actions *or* inactions, the Bible is clear that some of our "problems" result from the hands of our wise, loving Father God who intentionally orchestrates or puts us into such situations.

Why would God do this? From a close study of the Bible, we can learn a number of God's reasons:

- To bring us closer to Him
- To strengthen our trust and faith in God
- To purify us of sin in our lives
- To discipline (train, not punish) us
- To weed out those from His Church who are insincere
- To accomplish His greater purpose
- To give us a testimony we can share with other
- To enable us to walk with compassion with others in the same situation
- To bring God honor and glory

One of the most insightful examples of how God uses crises in our lives to accomplish His purposes can found in the book of Exodus. While God tempts no one (Jam. 1:13), He will lead us into difficult situations as a test to reveal what choices we will make. In the following scripture passage, God commands Moses to deliberately lead His people into a trap:

> "Tell the Israelites to turn back and encamp near Pi Hahiroth, between Migdol and the sea. They are to encamp by the sea, directly opposite Baal Zephon. Pharaoh will think, 'The Israelites are wandering around the land in confusion, hemmed in by the desert.' And I will harden Pharaoh's heart, and he will pursue them. But I will gain glory for myself through Pharaoh and all his army, and the Egyptians will know that I am the Lord." (Exod. 14:2-4)

While God's main purpose was to enable the final defeat of the Egyptian army, God didn't clue in His people the Israelites as to why they soon found themselves trapped between Pharaoh's approaching, avenging army and the Red Sea with nowhere to go. So, the Israelites did what we Christians likewise often do best today: freak out, scream, moan, grumble, and complain to everyone around.

The Israelites, like us today, did everything except pray, relax, have faith in God, and trust that He had a better plan through it all. Of course, God did have a great plan. At the last minute, He parted the Red Sea, and His people safely crossed through their major crisis on dry ground. This had been God's plan from the beginning. He didn't need the freaking out part to make this happen. He only needed faith and trust from His people.

In the book of Hebrews, God shared another of His reasons for why He allows tough times to befall us:

> Endure hardship as discipline; God is treating you as his children. For what children are not disciplined by their father? ... God disciplines us for our good, in order that we may share in his holiness. No discipline seems pleasant at the time, but painful. Later on, however, it produces a harvest of righteousness and peace for those who have been trained by it. Therefore, strengthen your feeble arms and weak knees. (Heb. 12:7, 9-12)

Because God's discipline is intended for our own good, He asks us to not only accept His discipline but to actually be happy about it when we face trials:

> Consider it pure joy, my brothers and sisters, whenever you face trials of many kinds, because you know that the testing of your faith produces *perseverance*. Let perseverance *finish its work* so that you may be *mature and complete*, not lacking anything. (Jam. 1:2-3, emphasis added)

This is why our Lord commends those of His servants who pass His testing and trying process without growing weary or giving up:

> [Jesus speaking to His Church at Ephesus] You have *persevered* and have *endured hardships* for my

name, and *have not grown weary.* (Rev. 2:3, emphasis added)

Blessed is the one who perseveres under trial because, *having stood the test,* that person will receive the crown of life that the Lord has promised to those who love him. (Jam. 1:12, emphasis added)

Here is a closing scripture passage that is worth pondering:

Even though I walk through the darkest valley,
I will fear no evil, for you are with me;
your rod and your staff, they comfort me.
(Psa. 23:4)

Amen! If you agree, pray this prayer:

I love and trust You, my Father God, that where you lead me is for my own best good and Your greater purposes. Refine me in Your fire and make me pure and white as snow in the name of your Son, Jesus.

Be blessed today!

83

Mastering Your Crisis (Part 3)

How to Use Your Faith in a Crisis

MANY TIMES, GOD'S PEOPLE SUCCESSFULLY maintain a certain amount of faith in the Lord although in the middle a crisis. However, we often turn around and manage to undermine both our faith and God's blessings with our negative, gloomy words.

In this devotional, we will see that what we believe in our hearts and *speak* with our lips will directly determine what God gives to us.

Let's start by carefully and prayerfully studying these three scriptures:

> The tongue has the power of life and death,
> and those who love it will eat its fruit.
> (Prov. 18:21)

> If you declare with your mouth, "Jesus is Lord," and believe in your heart that God raised him from the dead, you will be saved. For it is with your heart that you believe and are justified, and it is with your *mouth* that you profess your faith and are saved. (Rom. 10:9-10, emphasis added)

It is written: "I believed; therefore I have *spoken*." Since we have that same spirit of faith, we also believe and therefore *speak*. (2 Cor. 4:13, emphasis added)

In other words, what we say about the problems we are going through will result in us either blessing or cursing ourselves. It's our choice.

Let's examine a powerful example of this in the Bible. Notice the Lord's strong reaction to the ten spies' unbelief, who chose to let the giants and challenges their physical eyes saw overcome their faith in God and His promises for them (read the full story in your Bible):

The Lord said to Moses, "How long will these people treat me with contempt? How long will they refuse to believe in me, in spite of all the signs I have performed among them? ... So tell them, 'As surely as I live, declares the Lord, I will do to you the very thing I heard you *say*: ... Not one of you will enter the land I swore with up-lifted hand to make your home, except Caleb son of Jephunneh and Joshua son of Nun.'" (Num. 14:11, 28, 30, emphasis added)

My dear friends, notice that what the ten spies *spoke* was exactly what they received from God. Ten spies *said* they could not take the land, so they didn't and died in the wilderness. Though, two of the spies *said* they could, so they did and conquered the land (Caleb and Joshua).

What each person believed in his heart and spoke out loud with his lips for others to hear was exactly what each person subsequently received from God. Each person determined his own fate with what he said.

Here is another vivid example from God's Word that illustrates this critical principle:

> [David said to King Saul,] "Your servant has killed both the lion and the bear; this uncircumcised Philistine will be like one of them, because he has defied the armies of the living God. The Lord who rescued me from the paw of the lion and the paw of the bear will rescue me from the hand of this Philistine." (1 Sam. 17:36-37)

David won his victory over Goliath before his fight with the giant even started because of David's bold proclamation of his faith in his heart spoken out loud with his lips for *everyone* to hear, including his family (brothers) and the king of the land.

A final scripture:

> Do not let any unwholesome talk come out of your mouths, but *only* what is helpful for building others up according to their needs, that it may benefit those who listen. (Eph. 4:29, emphasis added)

How often do we follow this scripture? Does what we say around others glorify God and benefit those around us, or does what we say dishonor God, depress others intentionally or otherwise, or tear them down?

We must learn to speak into existence that for which we are believing God. Our faith must be demonstrated audibly. Specifically, we must ...

- Believe God's promises from His Word that He is with us always and has our best good in mind
- Proclaim our belief out loud with our lips
- Act on our belief through faith

Finally, if you are accustomed to praying weak "God-bless-me" type prayers that can mean anything or nothing, begin learning to pray specifically and boldly. God's Word is clear from one end of the Bible to the other that God is pleased by His servants' faith. The bolder our faith is, the bigger His miracles become on our behalf.

To learn more about the subjects of bold faith, specific prayer, and how to use your faith to receive the miracle you need from God, carefully review the following devotionals, which can be located by using the table of contents:

- "God's Ten Conditions for His Miraculous Response to Our Prayers"
- "God Will Perform Miracles for You if You Will Ask"
- "Asking God Versus Rebuking Satan"
- "Overcoming Doubt that Can Hinder Your Faith"
- "Worthiness before God"
- "What We Say Will Make or Break Us"
- "Instant Miracle Healing Testimony"
- "Believing the Word of God at Face Value"
- "Personal Testimonies Demonstrating Faith for the Miraculous"
- "How to Get a Pay Raise or a Better Job"

Be blessed in the name of Jesus!

84

Glimpse of the End of the World

[Jesus said,] "Heaven and earth will pass away, but my words will never pass away."

—Matthew 24:35

ON SATURDAY MORNING, JULY 28, 2012, the Lord gave me a vision of the end of this world.

Lying beside my sleeping wife after a time of personal Bible study, I began listening to praise and worship music with earbuds in my ears and a blindfold over my eyes in a manner similar to what I have written about previously (see "Fire of the Living God Manifested in Us Parts 1 and 2"). Fully awake as I turned over, it suddenly was as if my eyes had unexpectedly opened despite the blindfold over my eyes. Inexplicably, I found myself looking out through the window of our bedroom toward the west. Confused as to what was happening, I squeezed my eyes shut hard and held them closed, but nothing happened. Brilliant daytime light continued to flood my eyes as I remained looking out the window just the same as before.

Still unaware of what was happening, my hand flew up to check my blindfold. In amazement, I found that my blindfold was still in place over my eyes. I placed my arm tightly over my blindfold and rolled over in bed to face away from the window with my eyes tightly shut. The scene still did not change. I remained looking out through our bedroom window in bright sunshine toward the west, just the same as before.

At this point, I realized that the Lord had taken me into a vision in a manner I had not previously experienced, which is why I did not recognize it. Through the Holy Spirit, I asked the Lord why He was showing to me the familiar scenes of residences and buildings that I knew well from seeing those same scenes every day from my bedroom window.

As if in reply, only a hundred feet from me, a massive geyser of fire suddenly erupted out of the ground with a blast of tremendous force, thundering upward into the sky. The geyser of fire was about forty feet across and many hundreds of feet into the air. The buildings nearest me were blown apart as the collapsed debris instantly ignited in a raging inferno.

As my mind struggled to comprehend the meaning of the horrific scene in front of me, dozens of new fiery geysers blasted into the air all around me. They were quickly joined by hundreds and soon countless thousands of fiery geysers stretching past the horizon. Buildings, trees, forests, and everything else that was visible were all soon enveloped by towering, billowing sheets of flames as the fireballs merged together to form a raging sea of fire. As the vision began to fade, the smoky, dim red sky was blotted out by enormous flames that stretched as far as my eyes could see.

Despite the violent catastrophe erupting all around me, I felt no heat or fear. Instead, I only felt sad recognition that God's judgments were just and long delayed.

When the vision ended, I arose out of bed and went over to the window. Looking toward the west, I saw the same peaceful, serene scene I had always seen. Yet, this time, it was different. I knew like never before that this lovely place would one day be consumed in fiery flames.

All we hold so dear and precious now and hold on to so tightly will soon pass away.

The End of All Things

As the Lord had asked me to do previously (see "A Glimpse of Heaven"), I have attempted to do my best here to explain what the Lord showed me. God's coming judgments on the earth and the end of the world are coming as we know from scripture:

> But the day of the Lord will come like a thief. The heavens will disappear with a roar; the elements will be destroyed by fire, and the earth and everything done in it will be laid bare ... and the elements will melt in the heat. (2 Pet. 3:10, 12b)

How should we prepare for the coming end of the world? The Apostle Peter provided the answer in the next verses:

> Since everything will be destroyed in this way, what kind of people ought you to be? You ought to live holy and godly lives ... So then, dear friends, since you are looking forward to this,

make every effort to be found spotless, blameless
and at peace with him. (2 Pet. 3:11, 14)

This brings up a good question: Should we be fearful as
the end of the world approaches? Jesus Himself provided
the answer for us:

> [Jesus said,] "There will be signs in the sun,
> moon and stars. On the earth nations will be in
> anguish ad perplexity at the roaring and tossing
> of the sea. People will faint from terror apprehen-
> sive of what is coming upon the world, for the
> heavenly bodies will be shaken. At that time they
> will see the Son of Man coming in a cloud with
> power and great glory. When these things begin
> to take place, stand up and lift up your heads be-
> cause your redemption is drawing near."
> (Luke 21:25-27)

We have our Savior's command to stand and lift our
heads, because our redemption is near. Jesus will return to
Earth before many of us are ready for Him to do so (read the
story of the ten wise and foolish virgins in Matthew 25:1-
13). First and foremost, let's stay prepared daily as none of
us are promised tomorrow. Finally, let us act on what we
know by redoubling our efforts to warn our family, friends,
and others around us and lead them to Christ.

Go set a captive of Satan free today in the name of Jesus!
Be blessed.

*(See also the devotional lesson, "A Glimpse of Heaven" in this
book.)*

85

How to Draw Close to God

ONE WAY A BELIEVER WHO wishes to draw close to God can do so is to start by realizing just how close God already is to us. How can we do this? By mediating on the Word of God and allowing the Holy Spirit to change the way we think about God and His presence.

No matter how many times I have read Psalm 139 before, this chapter of the Bible continues to amaze and thrill me every time I read it. Although you may have read Psalm 139 before, this time, I urge you to read, stop, and mediate on the meaning of each of the following verses before continuing on to the next verse. As you contemplate each verse, consider not only its meaning but whether or not this is how you view God's presence during the average workday. Consider carefully:

> You have searched me, Lord, and you know me.
> You know when I sit and when I rise; you per-
> ceive my thoughts from afar.
> You discern my going out and my lying down;
> you are familiar with all my ways.
> Before a word is on my tongue
> you, Lord, know it completely …

Where can I go from your Spirit? Where can I
flee from your presence?
If I go up to the heavens, you are there; if I make
my bed in the depths, you are there.
If I rise on the wings of the dawn, if I settle on
the far side of the sea,
even there your hand will guide me, your right
hand will hold me fast.
If I say, "Surely the darkness will hide me and
the light become night around me,"
even the darkness will not be dark to you; the
night will shine like the day, for darkness is
as light to You. (Psa. 139:1-4, 7-12)

(Please read this full chapter in your Bible.)

Despite being amazed by these verses every time I read
them from childhood, I did not apply their meaning to my
life until soon after I started Bible college in 2011. For whatever reason, despite these scripture passages I still thought
of God as being far away from me personally. I'm not sure
now what I thought before, except that although I was a
born-again Christian the nearness of God's presence was
seldom real or meaningful to me then. God's Word had little
impact on my day-to-day thoughts, words, and conduct.
God generally seemed just too far away or "not real"
enough to me on any average day of my life to make a meaningful difference—beyond the basics of being a committed
Christian—until the fall of that year.

That's when God opened my eyes to the supernatural
world that is happening all around each of us at this very
moment. When God opened my eyes, I discovered firsthand

for myself that God closely watches everything we think and do at all times.

Once I finally understood the magnitude and reality of the supernatural battle that goes on endlessly around each of us, for several weeks afterward I was very nearly overpowered by this knowledge. It was almost too much. However, from that point on, it changed everything in terms of how I view God and interact with Him.

Since then, I no longer verbally raise my voice or look up into the heavens in an unconscious effort to reach a God who is far away. Instead, I now quietly speak to the almighty God and His Son who through the power of the Holy Spirit live within and around me at all times. The reality of God's presence has changed everything.

My friends, God literally lives within His believers and His angels surround us, just as He says and indicates in many places throughout His Word. Below is one such scripture passage. In reference to Abraham, Moses, and many more of God's people who have died and proceeded before us to heaven, the writer of Hebrews said,

> Therefore, since we are surrounded by such a great cloud of witnesses, let us throw off everything that hinders and the sin that so easily entangles. And let us run with perseverance the race marked out for us, fixing our eyes on Jesus, the pioneer and perfecter of faith. For the joy set before him he endured the cross, scorning its shame, and sat down at the right hand of the throne of God. Consider him who endured such opposition from sinners, so that you will not grow weary and lose heart. In your struggle

against sin, you have not yet resisted to the point
of shedding your blood. (Heb. 12:1-4)

In other words, Christ paid too high of a price for us,
and too many witnesses are watching us now for us to go
on messing up in life. Let's get it together. Let's toughen up
our thinking and actions in our ongoing battle against sin
and wickedness. We *can* overcome and we *can* draw near to
God because God is already near to us. Understanding the
reality of His abiding presence will change everything if we
will let it. Consider the words of Jesus:

> Here I am! I stand at the door and knock. If any-
> one hears my voice and opens the door, I will
> come in and eat with that person, and they with
> me. (Rev. 3:20)

By faith, understand today that Jesus is within you,
right now at this very moment. Pray this prayer, and mean
it from your heart:

> Father God, forgive me for not understanding
> the reality of your presence within me and
> around me at all times. Forgive me for being so
> distracted and tempted by the things of this
> world even though You have been standing right
> in front of me, watching everything I do. In the
> name of Your Son, Jesus, I commit to being aware
> from now on of Your abiding presence in and
> with me at all times.

It is very hard to intentionally sin when you are fully
aware that the eternal God of the universe and many other

witnesses both good and evil are carefully watching you to see what you do.

Go and live the overcoming life that Jesus wants for each of us. You are victorious and blessed today in the name of Jesus!

86

Seeking God's Help First

FROM THE STORY OF KING ASA of Judah, we can learn a valuable lesson for ourselves today:

> In the thirty-ninth year of his reign Asa was afflicted with a disease in his feet. Though his disease was severe, even in his illness he did not seek help from the Lord, but only from the physicians. (2 Chron. 16:12)

From the context, it is clear God wants us to seek His help for everything, even for relatively minor illnesses. But so often, we don't or won't, and we instead seek to take care of our problems our own way.

This is true not just with physical healing but with pretty much everything else as well. In fact, we can even manage to do things our own way while we are doing what God Himself asked us to do.

Huh? How is this possible? Let's examine the story of Joshua and his capture of the city of Ai.

In Joshua 7:1-12, Joshua and the armies of Israel were pumped after just having captured the city of Jericho where God supernaturally toppled the walls for them. Fresh off their easy victory, Joshua and his army turned their sights to the nearby, tiny city of Ai. Thinking it would be a cake-walk to capture such a tiny city, especially when God had already previously told them to capture the entire land of Canaan including the tiny city of Ai, Joshua made two serious mistakes we can learn a lot from today:

1. Joshua did not consult with God again to specifically ask for His guidance anew that day before battle.
2. Joshua sent only a small portion of his army against the enemy, instead of leading his entire army into battle.

Notice their thought process going into battle:

When [Joshua's spies] returned to Joshua, they said, "Not all the army will have to go up against Ai. Send two or three thousand men to take it and do not weary the whole army, for only a few people live there." So about three thousand went up; but they were routed by the men of Ai. (Josh. 7:3-4)

Had Joshua specifically asked for God's help that day prior to undertaking the work of God, Joshua would have learned that God had refused to bless them until serious sin in the camp had been rooted out. (A man named Achan had stolen merchandise that belonged to God.) After that sin in the camp was discovered and rooted out, Joshua then learned that God did not approve of his prior battle plan of sending only a small portion of his army:

Then the Lord said to Joshua, "Do not be afraid; do not be discouraged. Take the whole army with you, and go up and attack Ai. For I have delivered into your hands the king of Ai, his people, his city and his land. You shall do to Ai and its king as you did to Jericho and its king ..." (Josh. 8:1-2)

In other words, even when we are doing the stated will of the Lord for our lives, we still need to consult with our God and Maker at every step of the way every day while doing so.

Now, let's fast-forward a number of generations to King Jehoshaphat of Judah, who faced the same situation that Joshua had many years before. Thankfully, King Jehoshaphat got it right:

[King Ahab of Israel] asked Jehoshaphat, "Will you go with me to fight against Ramoth Gilead?"

Jehoshaphat replied to the king of Israel, "I am as you are, my people as your people, my horses as your horses." But Jehoshaphat also said to the king of Israel, "First seek the counsel of the Lord." (1 Kings 22:4-5)

Even though an enemy nation had occupied a city of Israel that God had previously given to His people, King Jehoshaphat of Judah still sought the counsel of the Lord afresh before attempting to do the will of the Lord.

In closing, read again with fresh eyes the words of our Lord and Savior, Jesus, while He walked on this earth:

[Jesus said,] "But seek first his kingdom and his righteousness, and all these things will be given to you as well." (Matt. 6:33)

"All these things" means *everything*. Let's make a point every day to put God first in our day and consult Him all throughout our day. God will bless and lead us as we do so. For tips and pointers about how we should start our day every day, see the prior devotional lesson titled, "Putting God First in Our Day."

Be blessed today in all you do in the name of Jesus as you put God first in everything.

87

What to Do When You Don't Know What to Do

WE ALL HAVE HAD PLENTY of times in our lives when we have reached significant decision points and did not know what to do next, yet God remained silent. You may be going through such a time now.

What should we do when we encounter such times in our lives? Here are three helpful tips.

First, as always, our first reaction should be to prayerfully and carefully consult the Word of God for our answer:

> Your word is a lamp for my feet, a light on my
> path. (Psa. 119:105)

To the surprise of many Christians, the Bible contains far more answers to modern everyday problems than most of us have ever imagined. Speaking for myself, I find it rare that I cannot find any modern-day situation I encounter in the Bible.

So, after first trying your best with prayer to find your answer in the Bible yourself, consult with someone you know who studies the Bible extensively and has his or her own life in Biblical order.

Second, stop right away if you find yourself using rationalizing words such as "only," "little," "should," "just," "really," etc. Here are several examples of unwise mental rationalization:

- "I *really* don't see how this couldn't be a good thing."
- "I *just* need to do (whatever)."
- "It's *only* for (whoever or whatever)."
- "This TV show *only* has a *little* sex in it, so it *really* isn't *that* bad."
- "It's *only* $10 (or whatever price). What's wrong with that?"

Ask God to help you to catch yourself and stop your course of action whenever you use one of these rationalizing words. This is one way God can help you recognize a faulty decision in the making and assist you in learning to make wise decisions.

Third and last, if a decision simply must be made now and cannot wait any longer, use the wisdom that God has given to you to make the best decision you can under the circumstances. Then, start moving forward. As you move forward, pray that God supernaturally directs your steps.

Notice in the following scripture passage how God supernaturally changed the direction of the Apostle Paul and his companions as they moved forward in doing His work:

> Paul and his companions traveled throughout the region of Phrygia and Galatia, having been kept by the Holy Spirit from preaching the word in the province of Asia. When they came to the border of Mysia, they tried to enter Bithynia, but

the spirit of Jesus would not allow them to. So they passed by Mysia and went down to Troas. During the night Paul had a vision of a man of Macedonia standing and begging him, "Come over to Macedonia and help us." After Paul had seen the vision, we got ready at once to leave for Macedonia, concluding that God had called us to preach the gospel to them. (Acts 16:6-10)

The Apostle Paul and his companions reversed direction, concluding that they needed go in the opposite way. But it is important to notice that they continued moving, doing what they knew God had already given them to do until God specifically instructed them otherwise.

Those who have the infilling of the Holy Spirit within them have a significant advantage in this regard if they have learned to hear His voice. The Word of God and the Holy Spirit will not allow us to go too far off course before God corrects our steps. If you are a Christian but have not yet received the infilling of the Holy Spirit within you and would like to learn more, see my three-part devotional series titled "Gift of the Holy Spirit (Parts 1-3)."

I pray that the Lord will supernaturally order your steps in all you do. Be blessed today in the name of Jesus!

88

Faith for the Impossible (Part 1)

As Christian believers, we ask God to forgive us of our sins and we expect Him to do so. We know that God will do so because, in God's Word, He has promised us that He will forgive us if we ask Him.

Yet, strangely, many of us don't expect God to heal us despite that God has promised to us in His Word that He will heal us if we ask ... exactly the same way He promises to forgive us if we ask.

So, why do we believe one of God's promises and not the other?

Our error occurs because we have somehow come to believe that it requires a lot of faith to ask God to heal us, but only a little faith to ask God to forgive us of our sins. But is our view accurate? What if miraculous healing does not require a lot of faith? What if it requires only a little faith?

Let's take a closer look at how God views the forgiveness of sin versus miraculous healing. In the following scripture passage, Jesus appears to have equated miraculous physical healing as requiring the same level effort to God as the forgiveness of sins:

[Jesus said,] "Which is easier: to say to this para-
lyzed man, 'Your sins are forgiven,' or to say,
'Get up, take your mat and walk'? But I want you
to know that the Son of Man has authority on
earth to forgive sins." So he said to the man, "I
tell you, get up, take your mat and go home." He
got up, took his mat and walked out in full view
of them all … (Mark 2:9-12a)

This helps to explain why, in the next scripture, Jesus
said that only a small amount of faith is needed for God to
do miracles on our behalf:

Jesus replied, "Because you have so little faith.
Truly I tell you, if you have faith as small as a
mustard seed, you can say to this mountain,
'Move from here to there,' and it will move.
Nothing will be impossible for you."
(Matt. 17:20)

By keeping in mind that to God the same level of effort
is required on His part to forgive our sins and miraculously
heal us, this will help us understand Jesus' statement that
faith the size of a mustard seed is all that is needed to move
mountains. We have been putting a bigger burden on ourselves than actually has been required of us by God. If Satan
can lie to us that a lot of faith is needed when it isn't, we
will, of course, fall short of our own false standard every
time and therefore needlessly falter in our request to God
for our miracle.

Because only a small amount of faith is needed according to the Word of God, from now on don't let Satan turn
your requests into a mountain. We only need a little faith.

Faith isn't a feeling, but rather a choice we must make every day and every time we pray. We only need to have faith that the promises of God in His Word are true. That's all the faith we need for miraculous healing or for any other miracle that we need.

Keeping this understanding fresh in our minds, let's read this promise of Jesus with new eyes:

> [Jesus said,] "I will do whatever you ask in my name, so that the Father may be glorified in the Son. You may ask me for anything in my name, and I will do it." (John 14:12-14)

My friends, the key to bold faith for the impossible is to learn to ignore how we feel and, instead, only *act* on what the Word of God says:

> [We] receive from him *anything* we ask, because we keep His commands and do what pleases Him. (1 John 3:22, emphasis added)

It has nothing to do with how we *feel*, but rather with our faith that the Word of God is true[1]. I *know* God is listening to me, and I *know* He will answer my requests. Why? Simply because God said He would in His Word ... not because I "feel" that way or because I know it any other way. My feelings about the matter are irrelevant. I make the intentional choice to let only what God's Word says count when I pray. God said He would, and I believe Him. That's all the faith that's needed.

The kind of faith that moves the heart of God to perform on-the-spot miracles on our behalf is the bold faith that *knows* God is listening and *knows* God will respond to our prayer simply *because* He said He would in His Word. The type of faith that merely *hopes* God is listening and *hopes* God will respond isn't actually faith at all. That kind of "faith" will produce no answers to such prayers.

Meditate and think on these things. In the next devotional lesson, we will visit again this book's topic of building our faith for the impossible. Be blessed today in the mighty name of Jesus!

---

[1]See also in this book "God's Ten Conditions for His Miraculous Response to Our Prayers" and "How to Pray for Miraculous Healing (Parts 1–3)"

89

Faith for the Impossible
(Part 2)

IN THE PREVIOUS DEVOTIONAL READING, we learned that believing for the miraculous physical healing of ourselves and others doesn't require a lot of faith; rather, it only requires a little faith that God's promises in His Word the Bible are true. But let's go even further today. I would like to share with you something that works wonders for me, even though I recognize that what works for me may not work for you, and vice versa. So this is a bit of a long shot. Here goes.

Big Miracles

I often like to think about the really big miracles God used to do in the Old Testament days ... incredible miracles like the 10 plagues falling on Egypt or God parting the Red Sea so that the Israelites could cross over on dry ground. God required Moses to have *lot* of faith ... or so it seems to me by comparison anyway.

My faith is strengthened by such contemplations because I realize in comparison just how little faith God requires of me at the present time (I often wonder what God has for me in the future and I pray to grow my faith to be prepared.) This type of backward thinking may not help you, but for me, meditating on God's Word in this way helps to strengthen my resolve to still higher heights to use faithfully the little faith that God has blessed me to have now.

Here's a case in point. Let's take a look at an amazing, great big miracle in the Word of God that blows my mind every time I think of it:

> [God said to Moses, "Tell the people,] 'Now the Lord will give you meat, and you will eat it. You will not eat it for just one day, or two days, or five, ten or twenty days, but for a whole month— until it comes out of your nostrils and you loathe it ...'"
>
> But Moses said, "Here I am among six hundred thousand men on foot, and you say, 'I will give them meat to eat for a whole month!' Would they have enough if flocks and herds were slaughtered for them? Would they have enough if all the fish in the sea were caught for them?"
>
> The Lord answered Moses, "Is the Lord's arm too short? Now you will see whether or not what I say will come true for you ..."
>
> Now a wind went out from the Lord and drove quail in from the sea. It scattered them up to two cubits deep all around the camp, as far as a day's walk in any direction. All that day and night and all the next day the people went out and gathered quail. No one gathered less than ten homers. (Num. 11:18-23, 31-32)

By my calculation, this was millions of tons of quail birds stretching over twenty miles in every direction. As God told Moses in verse 23, "Is the Lord's arm too short? Now you will see whether or not what I say will come true for you." What an immense miracle!

Here's another example from the Bible. I often think about Abraham and Sarah:

> Then one of [the angels] said, "I will surely return to you about this time next year, and Sarah your wife will have a son."
>
> Now Sarah was listening at the entrance to the tent, which was behind him. Abraham and Sarah were already very old, and Sarah was past the age of childbearing …
>
> Then the Lord said to Abraham, "Why did Sarah laugh and say, 'Will I really have a child, now that I am old?' *Is anything too hard for the Lord?* I will return to you at the appointed time next year, and Sarah will have a son."
> (Gen. 18:10-11, 13-14, emphasis added)

And she did. Jesus did say that *nothing* will be impossible for us:

> Jesus replied, "Because you have so little faith. Truly I tell you, if you have faith as small as a mustard seed, you can say to this mountain, 'Move from here to there,' and it will move. *Nothing will be impossible for you.*" (Matt. 17:20, emphasis added)

I often think that we can either choose to believe what Jesus said, or we can choose to believe what Satan says. Pick one. Our decision really is that simple.

Fear Not

As discussed yesterday, faith is a decision we make, not a feeling. Specifically, faith is a *decision* we must make to believe what the Word of God says above and beyond what our feelings and physical senses are telling us.

However, we are instructed hundreds of times throughout the Bible to "do not fear" in the first place. Here is the kind of confidence that God wants for each and every one of us:

> Though an army besiege me, my heart will not
> fear;
> though war break out against me, even then I
> will be confident. (Psa. 27:3)

In the end, faith for God to do the impossible comes down to a willing decision we must make every day to believe the Word of God above everything else. Today's faith will not work for tomorrow. Instead, each day, we must arise and choose to have faith in the Word of God and God's promises all over again, or else believe the lies of the enemy. I pray that we will choose to have faith in God's promises.

Be blessed today in the Name of Jesus.

90

Healing Through the Holy Spirit

AS PREVIOUSLY DISCUSSED IN LESSON 20, "God's Ten Conditions for His Miraculous Response to Our Prayers," when we pray in accordance with God's Will, God gives us what we ask for. Here is this promise in scripture:

> This is the confidence we have in approaching God: that *if we ask anything according to his will, he hears us.* And if we know that he hears us—whatever we ask—we know that we have what we asked of him. (1 John 5:14-15, emphasis added)

So how can we know we are praying in agreement with the will of God? Specifically, how do we know that our prayers for the healing of others are in agreement with God's will for those individuals? First, for starters we know that the will of God is revealed in His written Word the Bible:

> Very truly I tell you, whoever believes in me will do the works I have been doing, and they will do even greater things than these, because I am going to the Father. *And I will do whatever You ask in*

*My name, so that the Father may be glorified in the
Son. You may ask Me for anything in My name, and
I will do it.* (John 14:12-13, emphasis added)

Yet frustratingly enough, when we pray for the healing
of others in faith according to this scripture, over time we
observe that only some of the people we pray for are healed.
How is this possible?

The answer to this important question can be found in
the words of Jesus. Acting as our example during His ministry here on earth, listen to what Jesus said was the source
of His actions here on earth. Let's learn how everything Jesus did was guided by God the Father:

Jesus gave them this answer: "Very truly I tell
you, the Son can do nothing by himself; *he can do
only what he sees his Father doing, because whatever
the Father does the Son also does. For the Father loves
the Son and shows him all he does.* Yes, and he will
show him even greater works than these, so that
you will be amazed." (John 5:19-20, emphasis
added)

Don't you believe that I am in the Father, and
that the Father is in me? The words I say to you I
do not speak on my own authority. *Rather, it is
the Father, living in me, who is doing his work.*
(John 14:10, emphasis added)

So, this becomes our next question. How did Jesus
know what the Father was saying and doing? How did Jesus know what say and what to do? As usual, the Word of
God gives us the answer:

For he (Jesus) is sent by God. *He speaks God's words, for God gives him the Spirit without limit.* (John 3:34 NLT, emphasis added)

Ah! Now we see! Jesus our example operated here on earth by the power of the Holy Spirit. It is the role of the Holy Spirit to teach us and guide in life, including as we pray for the healing of others as Jesus promised us that we would (see John 14:12-13 quoted previously above in this lesson). Notice:

But the Helper (Comforter, Advocate, Intercessor—Counselor, Strengthener, Standby), the Holy Spirit, whom the Father will send in My name [in My place, to represent Me and act on My behalf], *He will teach you all things. And He will help you remember everything that I have told you.* (John 14:26 Amplified Bible, emphasis added)

This is the constant work of the Holy Spirit, to show us how do the works of the Father. The Bible says, "We know not what to pray for," but that the Holy Spirit does:

In the same way, the Spirit helps us in our weakness. *We do not know what we ought to pray for,* but the Spirit Himself intercedes for us through wordless groans. And he who searches our hearts knows the mind of the Spirit, because the Spirit intercedes for God's people *in accordance with the will of God.* (Romans 8:26, emphasis added)

The closer we pay attention to the Holy Spirit and carefully follow His guidance, the more effectively we can do the works of our Father God and our Lord and Savior Jesus:

> Those who live according to the flesh have their minds set on what the flesh desires; *but those who live in accordance with the Spirit have their minds set on what the Spirit desires* ... For those who are led by the Spirit of God are the children of God. (Romans 8:5, 14, emphasis added)

> *And pray in the Spirit on all occasions with all kinds of prayers and requests.* With this in mind, be alert and always keep on praying for all the Lord's people. (Eph. 6:18, emphasis added)

> But you, dear friends, by building yourselves up in your most holy faith *and praying in the Holy Spirit*, keep yourselves in God's love as you wait for the mercy of our Lord Jesus Christ to bring you to eternal life. (Jude 1:20-21, emphasis added)

From experience, I can share with you that without the case-by-case guidance of the Holy Spirit directing our every word and action as we pray for the healing of others, as many as one-half of the people we pray for are healed. In these types of healings, those we pray for are largely being healed by their own faith, which is raised as a result our ministry and prayer for healing on their behalf (see Mark 5:24-32, Luke 17:11-19, and Matthew 15:21-28).

So how can we sharply increase our success rate so that many more people are healed? Answer: by carefully listening for and following the guidance of the Holy Spirit, just as Jesus did. If we carefully listen for the direction of Holy Spirit on a case-by-case basis, then He will instruct us *how*, often *when*, and even *where* to pray for someone's physical healing. It continually amazes me how varied is the Holy Spirit's leading in healing cases, often remarkably so.

We can see this fully illustrated in the life of Jesus. Notice how Jesus used wide array of different methods to heal different people who all suffered from the same physical condition (blindness), as Jesus was led by the Holy Spirit in each case individually (see John 9:1-6; Mark 8:22-26; Luke 18:35-43).

As examples from my own personal experience of years in the healing ministry, at times the Holy Spirit may instruct me *not* to immediately pray for someone, because that person has a condition which must be dealt with first, such as bitterness or unforgiveness toward God, or being knowingly and willingly oppressed or possessed by a demonic spirit.

At other times the Holy Spirit may instruct me to pray a specific prayer I have never prayed before, or to place my hands on the person in a particular way, or to prayerfully continue to wait on Him to give me further guidance. The Holy Spirit may direct me to go into intercessory prayer, or may raise more blocking issues which must be corrected one-by-one through prayer and personal ministry to that person (for a list of correctable obstacles to healing, see Lesson 20, "God's Ten Conditions for His Miraculous Response to Our Prayers").

As I listen carefully to and obey the Holy Spirit's instructions, the person I am praying for is healed. While this process often happens quickly, at times it may require a sustained period of pressing in, listening and acting on the information received. In especially tough cases, this process may require several hours to complete. Finally, unconfessed sin and divisions between leaders of a church may hinder their prayers for the sick, as is hinted in the scripture:

> Is anyone among you sick? Let them call the elders of the church to pray over them and anoint them with oil in the name of the Lord. And the prayer offered in faith will make the sick person well; the Lord will raise them up. If they have sinned, they will be forgiven. *Therefore confess your sins to each other and pray for each other so that you may be healed.* The prayer of a righteous person is powerful and effective. (James 5:14-16, emphasis added)

And even then, from time to time someone still may not be healed. It is conceivable this could be because of a lack of sufficient faith on our part, or that it might even be the Will of the Lord not to heal that individual at that time or in that way.

Here are two examples of this from scripture. In the first, notice what Jesus had to say about a man who was born blind:

> As he (Jesus) went along, he saw a man blind from birth. His disciples asked him, "Rabbi, who sinned, this man or his parents, that he was born blind?"

"Neither this man nor his parents sinned," said Jesus, *"but this happened so that the works of God might be displayed in him."* (John 9:1-2, emphasis added)

Next, notice how the Apostle Paul was not healed of what appears to have been an ailment of some kind in his physical body which troubled him:

In order to keep me from becoming conceited, I was given a thorn in my flesh, a messenger of satan, to torment me. Three times I pleaded with the Lord to take it away from me. *But he said to me, "My grace is sufficient for you, for my power is made perfect in weakness."* Therefore I will boast all the more gladly about my weaknesses, so that Christ's power may rest on me. That is why, for Christ's sake, I delight in weaknesses, in insults, in hardships, in persecutions, in difficulties. For when I am weak, then I am strong.
(2 Cor. 12:7b-10, emphasis added)

In conclusion, here's what I know works for sure: the more I pray in tongues, the more frequently and clearly I hear the voice of the Holy Spirit. And the more I clearly hear the voice of the Holy Spirit, the more I am able to do the works that Jesus did, just as He said we would in John 14:12-13.

For much more information about the Holy Spirit, including how to receive the Spirit to the overflowing point and how pray in the Spirit, see "Gift of the Holy Spirit (Parts 1–3)" in this book.

Be blessed in Jesus Name as you do the works that He did!

For additional assistance with difficult healing cases, see the following related material in this book:

- Lessons 69–71, "How to Pray for Miraculous Healing (Parts 1-3)"
- Lesson 20 "God's Ten Conditions for His Miraculous Response to Our Prayers"
- Lesson 72 "Demonstrating Our Faith to Enable Our Miracle"
- Lesson 76, "Breaking the Cycle of Unworthiness and Unanswered Prayer"

Stay in Touch

To receive notification of future updates to this devotional and other publications as they are released by Life of Faith in Christ Ministries, sign up to join our email list at our website at: www.lifeoffaithinchrist.org.

We welcome you to follow us on Facebook at:
www.facebook.com/LifeofFaithinChrist/

Join us on Twitter at:
twitter.com/LifeFaithChrist

Finally, you may also email us at:
info@lifeoffaithinchrist.org

...or write us via postal mail to our mailing address:

Life of Faith in Christ Ministries:
2211 Rayford Rd. Ste. 111-308
Spring, Texas USA 77386

Phone:
United States: (281) 719-9345
International: +1-281-719-9345

Printed in Great Britain
by Amazon

43808980R00179